FLORIDA
Treasures

FCAT Format
Weekly
Assessment

 Macmillan/McGraw-Hill

A

The McGraw·Hill Companies

Macmillan McGraw-Hill

Published by Macmillan/McGraw-Hill, of McGraw-Hill Education, a division of The McGraw-Hill Companies, Inc.,
Two Penn Plaza, New York, New York 10121.

Printed in the United States of America

1 2 3 4 5 6 7 8 9 005 10 09 08 07

Contents

Unit 1

Unit 2

Unit 3

© Macmillan/McGraw–Hill

Unit 4

Unit 5

Unit 6

© Macmillan/McGraw–Hill

Introduction to the Weekly Assessment

The Weekly Assessment is designed to assess your students' mastery of the skills taught throughout the week. The test questions use formats your students will encounter on the Florida Comprehensive Assessment Test (FCAT) in grade 5. The test includes questions that cover the following areas:

- Vocabulary Strategies
- Reading Comprehension
- Spelling
- Grammar, Mechanics, and Usage

Purpose of the Weekly Assessment

Each week, there will be a new passage for students to read. The passage will be either fiction or nonfiction, depending on the genre of the core selection for the week. It will be followed by 15 questions that cover the skills for the week.

Providing students with a new read allows you to assess how well they have mastered the skills for the week. When students apply what they have learned, you can evaluate the degree of mastery they have achieved.

Using the Results to Inform Instruction

Use the results of the Weekly Assessment as a formative assessment tool to help monitor each student's progress. Information gathered by evaluating the results of this assessment also can be used to diagnose specific strengths and weaknesses of your students. If you use Weekly Assessment scores to help determine report card grades, then you can consider the tests to be summative assessments as well.

How to Use and Administer the Weekly Assessment

Each Weekly Assessment consists of 14 multiple-choice questions and 1 constructed-response question. The format and length of the test is the same each week. You may want to explain each section of the test to students the first time you administer it.

- For the multiple-choice questions, students should circle the letter next to the best answer. (If you are using the separate Answer Sheet, direct students to fill in the bubble for the best answer. Remind students to fill in the bubble completely for each answer.)

- For the constructed-response questions, students should write their answers in the space provided on the page. (If you are using the separate Answer Sheet, direct students to write their answers on the back of the Answer Sheet.)

The **Answer Keys** to score the tests can be found on **pages 369–377.**

Answer Sheets and **sample score points for the constructed-response questions** can be found on the **web site** at http://www.macmillanmh.com.

General Procedures

Before the test: Distribute copies of the Weekly Assessment and the Answer Sheet, if you choose to use one.

Directions: Say: *Write your name and the date on the cover of your test booklet.* (If you are using the separate Answer Sheet, say: *Write your name and the date at the top of the Answer Sheet.*) When all students are finished, say: *Open the booklet to page 2. You will read a passage. Then carefully read the questions that follow. For each multiple-choice question, read all of the answer choices. Then circle the letter next to the best answer.* (If you are using the separate Answer Sheet, say: *Then fill in the bubble for the answer choice you think is correct. Fill in all answer bubbles completely. Do not mark outside the bubble.*) *For the constructed-response question, you will write your answer in the space provided on the page* (If you are using the separate Answer Sheet, say: *For the constructed-response question, you will write your answer on the back of the Answer Sheet.*) *When you finish the last question, close your booklet and put your pencil down. You may begin now.*

During the test: Monitor students' test-taking behavior to make sure that each student is following the directions and writing responses in the correct places. Answer questions about procedures and materials, but do not help students answer questions.

After the test: Before collecting the papers, make sure that students have written their names on the cover of the test booklet or at the top of the Answer Sheet.

Scoring Instructions

Using the Student Evaluation Charts

After each Weekly Assessment there is a Student Evaluation Chart. It lists all of the skills covered and the number of the question that assesses each skill.

- In the column labeled "Number Correct," fill in the point value for the questions answered correctly for each skill. Add the total number of points for correct responses and write the number for each subtest next to the total possible score.

- Add the scores for each skill (point value of the items answered correctly) to determine the total test score.

- To convert these raw test scores to percentages, see the **Scoring Chart** on the **inside back cover** of this book.

Multiple-choice questions are worth one point. Short-response questions are worth two points and extended-response questions are worth four points. Use the **Constructed-Response Rubrics** on **page 378** to help score the constructed-response questions.

Evaluating the Scores

The primary focus of the Weekly Assessment is to measure students' progress toward mastery of each skill. Scores that fall below the 80th percentile suggest that students require additional instruction before mastery of that skill can be achieved.

Evaluating the results of this assessment provides specific information about students' daily instructional needs. We recommend that you use these results for instructional planning and reteaching opportunities. Compare these results with your own observations of students' work and identify objectives that still need reinforcement. Incorporate these into your instructional plans for the coming week for individual, small-group, or whole-group instruction as indicated.

Tips for Taking the FCAT Format Weekly Assessment

Here are some tips to help you do your best. Keep these tips in mind when you answer the questions.

✓ Read the directions carefully. Ask your teacher to explain any directions you do not understand.

✓ Read the passages and questions very carefully. You may look back at a passage as often as you like.

✓ Answer the questions you are sure about first. If a question seems too difficult, skip it and go back to it later.

✓ Be sure to fill in the answer bubbles correctly. Do not make any stray marks around answer spaces.

✓ Think positively. Some questions may seem hard, but others will be easy.

✓ Check each answer to make sure it is the best answer for the question.

✓ Relax. Some people get nervous about tests. It's natural. Just do your best.

Directions for Taking the FCAT Format Weekly Assessment

This test contains 14 multiple-choice questions and 1 constructed-response question. A multiple-choice question is followed by several answer choices. Read all the answer choices under each question and decide which answer is correct. Circle the letter next to the answer choice you think is correct for each multiple-choice question. If you are using an Answer Sheet, fill in the bubble for the correct answer. For the constructed-response question, write your answer in the space provided on the page. If you are using an Answer Sheet, write your answer on the back of the Answer Sheet.

Name _____

Date _____

FCAT Format Weekly Assessment

TESTED SKILLS AND STRATEGIES

- **Vocabulary Strategies**
- **Reading Comprehension**
- **Spelling**
- **Grammar, Mechanics, and Usage**

Macmillan
McGraw-Hill

Read the story "The Big Contest" before answering Numbers 1 through 9.

The Big Contest

"We'll win this contest," José bragged to Aisha at recess.

"How?" Aisha asked. "Why did the fifth grade pick us to represent everyone in the Big Bake-Off? What are we supposed to do? What do we know about baking?"

"You don't give us enough credit," José said. "We're capable kids. We know how to follow directions, so using a recipe shouldn't be any problem at all. The contest has many different categories and divisions, and I've got a plan."

Suddenly, Aisha's memory went back to a day at recess last year. She saw herself listening to José's big plan. That one had gotten them into big trouble. They were thrown out of the contest altogether.

"Aisha, are you listening to me?" asked José.

Aisha shook herself back into the present and asked, "What's your plan?"

"We'll bake a gigantic cake. No one will bake a cake larger than ours! Our cake will be so huge that we'll get the prize for the biggest cake," he said.

Aisha said, "You know what, José? You're on to something! That's an excellent plan!"

The next day, Aisha and José went to the grocery store and bought the ingredients for their cake. At Aisha's house, they set everything on the counter and started working. "We'll bake a few cakes at a time. Then we'll put them together with a lot of frosting," Aisha said.

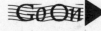

They poured, sifted, stirred, mixed, and baked. While one batch of cakes was in the oven, they started on the next. Much later, Aisha saw the luminous dial on the clock glowing. They had been so busy that they hadn't noticed how dark it had become. Cakes were everywhere, and the kids slumped against the kitchen counter in exhaustion. "My back hurts. I'll never stand up straight again," José moaned, as he put all the cakes on a big board. Aisha brushed strands of hair from her eyes. Then she started spreading the frosting. "This part of the cake is soggy," she said.

"So it's mushy," José said. "It will dry out by tomorrow. No one will notice."

The next day, with the help of Aisha's father and José's mother, the two kids took the huge cake to the school. They left it on one of the special tables set up in the cafeteria for the contest. It was surrounded by many smaller cakes.

GoOn ▶

That day felt like the longest school day ever. Finally it was the last period of the day—time for the contest to begin! All the students at the school went to the cafeteria. They watched as the judges tasted each of the cakes. José and Aisha saw the judges taste the other cakes and smile a lot. But they didn't taste the huge cake.

"This looks bad for us," Aisha whispered to José. "What's wrong with our cake? Why won't they even try a bite of it?"

"Don't worry, Aisha. We'll win," José said, almost but not quite so sure as he had been the day before.

"Look! The judging is over. I'm really nervous," Aisha said.

One of the judges cleared his throat and announced, "First prize for the biggest cake goes to . . ." All the fifth grade students held their breath. ". . . Aisha Thomas and José Mora, representing the fifth grade!"

"What did I tell you? It was inevitable that we would win," José said to Aisha with a smile. "I never doubted it for a minute!"

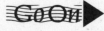

Student Name _____

**Now answer Numbers 1 through 9 on your Answer Sheet.
Base your answers on the story "The Big Contest."**

1 Read this sentence from the story.

> **"The contest has many different categories and
> divisions, and I've got a plan."**

Which word in the sentence means about the SAME as
the word *categories*?

A. plan   **C.** different

B. contest   **D.** divisions

2 Read this sentence from the story.

> **"We'll bake a gigantic cake."**

Which word means almost the SAME as *gigantic*?

F. average

G. beautiful

H. delicious

I. enormous

3 Read these sentences from the story.

> **Much later, Aisha saw the luminous dial on the clock
> glowing. They had been so busy that they hadn't
> noticed how dark it had become.**

Which word in these sentences helps you understand the
meaning of *luminous*?

A. dial   **C.** noticed

B. clock   **D.** glowing

4 Read these sentences from the story.

> **Aisha brushed strands of hair from her eyes. Then she started spreading the frosting. "This part of the cake is soggy," she said.**

The word *soggy* means almost the SAME as

　F. firm.

　G. style.

　H. mushy.

　I. overcooked.

5 José plans to win the contest by

　A. using a secret ingredient in the cake.

　B. baking a cake for an unusual category.

　C. baking something that does not look like a cake.

　D. using much more frosting than normal on the cake.

6 What kind of person is José?

　F. quiet

　G. unsure

　H. confident

　I. impatient

© Macmillan/McGraw–Hill

7 What kind of person is Aisha?

    A. pushy

    B. fearful

    C. stubborn

    D. cooperative

8 The climax of the story takes place when

    F. José reveals his secret plan.

    G. José and Aisha shop for ingredients.

    H. José and Aisha bake the cake, but part of it is mushy.

    I. José and Aisha are waiting to hear whether they have won.

GO ON ▶

9 Where in the story does a flashback occur? Use details and information from the story to support your answer.

READ
THINK
EXPLAIN

_____

_____

_____

_____

_____

_____

_____

_____

_____

Go On ▶

Student Name _____

Read and answer questions 10–12 on your Answer Sheet.

10 Which word is spelled incorrectly?

    A. scan

    B. notch

    C. rough

    D. geuss

11 Read this sentence.

> **The stump was so <u>tough</u> and <u>rough</u> that the lumberjack just gave a <u>laff</u> and a <u>shrug</u> and did not try to remove it.**

Which underlined word is spelled incorrectly?

    F. laff

    G. shrug

    H. tough

    I. rough

12 Read this sentence.

> **The camper had to <u>fling</u> the blanket from the <u>damp</u> <u>cott</u> and put her <u>stuff</u> on the ground.**

Which underlined word is spelled incorrectly?

    A. cott

    B. fling

    C. stuff

    D. damp

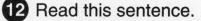

© Macmillan/McGraw-Hill

Student Name _____

Read and answer questions 13–15 on your Answer Sheet.

13 Read this sentence.

> **On Friday Luis and Michael went to the museum**

What is the BEST way to correct the sentence in the box?

  F. Change *and* to *or*.

  G. Add a period at the end.

  H. Add a question mark at the end.

14 Which sentence below is a command?

  A. Clean up the parks!

  B. What a beautiful bird!

  C. How can kids protect wildlife?

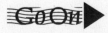

© Macmillan/McGraw-Hill

15 In which sentence below is all **punctuation** correct?

    F. Tranh, are you going to be on the basketball team.

    G. Ms. Alexander, our state senator, is going to visit our town!

    H. Do you want to go to the play on Friday, Saturday, or Sunday!

STOP

Student Name _____

Grade 5 • Unit 1 • Week 1
Student Evaluation Chart

Tested Skills	Number Correct	Percent Correct
Vocabulary Strategies: *Context clues: synonyms,*1, 3; *synonyms,* 2, 4	/4	%
Reading Comprehension: *Plot development: character, plot,* 5, 6, 7, 8	/4	%
Short response: *Plot development: character, plot,* 9	/2	%
Spelling: *Short vowels,* 10, 11, 12	/3	%
Grammar, Mechanics, and Usage: *Punctuate sentences,* 13, 15; *sentences,* 14	/3	%

Total Weekly Test Score	/16	%

	Correlations	
Item	FCAT Assessed Benchmarks*	New Sunshine State Standards
1	LA.A.1.2.3	LA.5.1.6.3
2	LA.A.1.2.3	LA.5.1.6.8
3	LA.A.1.2.3	LA.5.1.6.3
4	LA.A.1.2.3	LA.5.1.6.8
5	LA.E.1.2.2	LA.5.2.1.2
6	LA.E.1.2.2	LA.5.2.1.2
7	LA.E.1.2.2	LA.5.2.1.2
8	LA.E.1.2.2	LA.5.2.1.2
9	LA.E.1.2.2	LA.5.2.1.2
10		LA.5.3.4.1
11		LA.5.3.4.1
12		LA.5.3.4.1
13		LA.5.3.4.3
14		LA.5.3.4.3
15		LA.5.3.4.3

* See benchmarks and standards on pages 379–384.

Name _____

Date _____

FCAT Format Weekly Assessment

TESTED SKILLS AND STRATEGIES

- **Vocabulary Strategies**
- **Reading Comprehension**
- **Spelling**
- **Grammar, Mechanics, and Usage**

Macmillan
McGraw-Hill

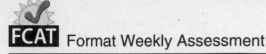

Read the story "Paul Bunyan and Babe the Blue Ox" before answering Numbers 1 through 9.

Paul Bunyan and Babe the Blue Ox

Paul Bunyan is an American legend and a truly original character. He was a giant lumberjack who did giant things.

Just how giant was he? Well, three hours after his birth, he weighed 80 pounds. And his fast rate of growth did not stop. After one week he had to wear his father's clothes. The amount of food he ate certainly helped him to grow so fast. For breakfast, he would eat 40 bowls of oatmeal at once.

Paul was enormously brave. One of his acts of bravery was to juggle a flaming fireball or two. This would always impress the people watching him.

Paul's special friend was an animal named Babe the Blue Ox. Paul had rescued Babe from drowning, and they had elected to stay together ever since. Babe, who was every bit as big as Paul, often traveled with Paul on his adventures. This unusual pair could always find excitement.

Sometimes, when they had a little free time, the two of them sauntered down to the golf course. Paul did not play golf the way most people do. His golf course was 30 miles wide. The sand pit stretched for acres, like a desert, and the water hazard was a huge lake. Because Paul used cannonballs for golf balls, only Babe was able to carry Paul's enormous golf bag.

© Macmillan/McGraw–Hill

Go On ►

Babe didn't play the game, but he would watch. Sometimes he would set up a little challenge for Paul. For example, the ox might tell Paul where to hit the ball and see if he could do it. Babe was a polite ox, but he knew how to get Paul riled up. And when Paul was riled up, big things could happen.

One day Babe challenged Paul to hit his ball a mile. Paul took a mighty swing, and the ball sailed nine-tenths of a mile—just a tenth of a mile too short. Paul was not at all happy. In fact, he was a little angry. Maybe it was because he had failed the challenge, or maybe it was because of Babe's quiet laugh afterwards. Whatever the reason, Paul stomped off without taking away his golf tee.

GO ON ▶

You may have seen it just off the local highway. A pair of eagles has commenced building their nest on it. Those eagles will be all finished in a few days.

At other times Paul would lose his golf balls in the huge lake. Babe the Blue Ox became skilled at diving down to retrieve those balls, and then he would wring them dry.

Speaking of that huge lake, Paul gave it its original name: Ox's Lake. But today you probably know it as Ox Lake in Minnesota.

Life for Paul Bunyan and Babe the Blue Ox wasn't just about having fun. When Babe and Paul weren't golfing, they were working at the logging campground. There they had many more adventures.

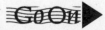

Student Name _____

**Now answer Numbers 1 through 9 on your Answer Sheet.
Base your answers on the story "Paul Bunyan and Babe
the Blue Ox."**

1 Read these sentences from the story.

> **Paul was enormously brave. One of his acts of
> bravery was to juggle a flaming fireball or two.**

Which clue can you use to define the word *fireball*?

A. Use the context clue *juggle*.

B. Break the word into its suffix and root word.

C. Break the word into its prefix and root word.

D. Break the word into two small words, *fire* and *ball*.

2 Read these sentences from the story.

> **You may have seen it just off the local highway. A pair
> of eagles has commenced building their nest on it.**

Which word means almost the SAME as *commenced*?

F. ended   **H.** decided

G. begun   **I.** completed

3 Read this sentence from the story.

> **Speaking of that huge lake, Paul gave it its original
> name: Ox's Lake.**

Which word means almost the SAME as *original*?

A. first   **C.** changed

B. natural   **D.** common

© Macmillan/McGraw–Hill

4 Read this sentence from the story.

> **When Babe and Paul were not golfing, they were working at the logging campground.**

The word *campground* means

F. a house in the woods.

G. a lightweight sleeping cot.

H. a meeting place for hikers.

I. an area where camping is allowed.

5 How did Paul and Babe meet?

A. Babe saved Paul's life.

B. Paul saved Babe's life.

C. Paul bought Babe at a fair.

D. Babe and Paul met on a golf course.

6 How does Babe help Paul?

F. by challenging Paul

G. by giving Paul advice

H. by finding Paul's golf tees

I. by carrying Paul's golf bag

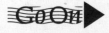

7 Why does Paul leave his golf tee behind?

    A. He thinks Babe is going to bring it.

    B. He wants eagles to build a nest on it.

    C. He has lost his ball at the bottom of a lake.

    D. He is upset that he did not hit the ball a mile.

8 Paul calls the lake Ox's Lake because

    F. Babe hit so many balls in it.

    G. Paul saved Babe from drowning in it.

    H. Paul wanted to name it after his friend.

    I. Babe dove into the lake to get golf balls.

Go On ▶

9 What is special about the golf course that Paul plays on? Use details from the story to support your answer.

READ
THINK
EXPLAIN

_____

_____

_____

_____

_____

_____

_____

_____

_____

Go On ▶

13 What is the complete predicate of sentence 1 ?

   F. recycling drive

   G. Lantana is having

   H. The town of Lantana

   I. is having a recycling drive

14 What is the subject of sentence 4 ?

   A. work at

   B. recycling drive

   C. Saturday afternoon

   D. Luisa, Tom, and Rae

15 In which sentence is all **punctuation** correct?

   F. sentence 2

   G. sentence 3

   H. sentence 5

   I. sentence 6

STOP

Grade 5 • Unit 1 • Week 2
Student Evaluation Chart

Tested Skills	Number Correct	Percent Correct
Vocabulary Strategies: *Compound words,* 1,4; *synonyms,* 2, 3	/4	%
Reading Comprehension: *Plot development: character, setting,* 5, 6, 7, 8	/4	%
Short response: *Plot development: character, setting,* 9	/2	%
Spelling: *Long vowels,* 10, 11, 12	/3	%
Grammar, Mechanics, and Usage: *Subjects and predicates,* 13, 14; *use commas in a series,* 15	/3	%
Total Weekly Test Score	**/16**	**%**

Correlations

Item	FCAT Assessed Benchmarks*	New Sunshine State Standards
1		LA.5.1.6.5
2	LA.A.1.2.3	LA.5.1.6.8
3	LA.A.1.2.3	LA.5.1.6.8
4		LA.5.1.6.5
5	LA.E.1.2.2	LA.5.2.1.2
6	LA.E.1.2.2	LA.5.2.1.2
7	LA.E.1.2.2	LA.5.2.1.2
8	LA.E.1.2.2	LA.5.2.1.2
9	LA.E.1.2.2	LA.5.2.1.2
10		LA.5.3.4.1
11		LA.5.3.4.1
12		LA.5.3.4.1
13		LA.5.3.4.4
14		LA.5.3.4.4
15		LA.5.3.4.3

* See benchmarks and standards on pages 379–384.

Name _____

Date _____

FLORIDA
Treasures

FCAT Format Weekly Assessment

TESTED SKILLS AND STRATEGIES

- Vocabulary Strategies
- Reading Comprehension
- Spelling
- Grammar, Mechanics, and Usage

Mc Graw Hill Macmillan
McGraw-Hill

Read the article "Desert Environments" before answering
Numbers 1 through 9.

Desert Environments

Deserts cover about one-fifth of Earth. Some deserts are sandy. Others are rocky. Yet all deserts have one major feature in common—lack of rainfall. Deserts are dry, desolate places. The desert landscape is harsh. Few large animals live in deserts. Few trees grow there, and the ones that do are not like most forest trees. Forest trees generally grow tall and straight. But desert trees are short, and they often have amazing shapes. The winds that buffet them twist the trees into these shapes.

There is animal and plant life even in the harsh desert climate.

The temperature in deserts can be hot or cold. The Sahara Desert in Africa gets very hot during the day but at night the temperature goes down. Deserts like this are called "hot" deserts. In contrast, the Gobi Desert in Asia is always cold, as are the deserts at the South Pole. These are called "cold" deserts.

Desert animals have special characteristics that allow them to adapt to their harsh settings. In hot deserts, some animals go on a quest for food early in the morning, the coolest time of the day. Early in the day roadrunners chase rattlesnakes and coyotes hunt for ground squirrels. During the heat of the day, many animals hide. Some hide under the ground, while others hide under rocks. At night, the temperature gets much cooler. Then the animals come out to find food. Scorpions and bats hunt for insects. Desert spiders as big as mice also hunt at night.

Animals in cold deserts have a different system. They hunt during the day when temperatures are slightly warmer. But the nights are very cold, and the animals take shelter.

Living conditions are harsh in a desert. Because food is never plentiful, most desert animals are small and skinny. How do desert animals survive with little or no food to eat? Some of them store fat in their bodies. For example, one type of desert lizard

Desert animals generally are not plump like the squirrels in a neighborhood. In a neighborhood, it is easy to find food.

GoOn ▶

stores fat in its large tail; it uses this fat when food is scarce. This is similar to some types of forest bears who store fat in their bodies during the summer. In the winter, when they hibernate, they have a reduced need for food. However, they still need some food. They get that food from their stored fat.

Deserts get very little rainfall. When there is a rainstorm, pools of water form on the ground. The animals drink as much water as they can. Yet some desert animals do not drink at all. They get all the water they need from the food they eat.

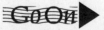

Student Name _____

**Now answer Numbers 1 through 9 on your Answer Sheet.
Base your answers on the article "Desert Environments."**

1 Read this sentence from the article.

> **Yet all deserts have one major feature in common—
> lack of rainfall.**

Which meaning of the word *major* is used In the sentence?

A. ma-jor (mā´ jər) *Adjective*. serious

B. ma-jor (mā´ jər) *Noun*. an academic subject

C. ma-jor (mā´ jər) *Noun*. an officer in the army

D. ma-jor (mā´ jər) *Adjective*. of great importance

2 Read this sentence from the article.

> **The winds that buffet them twist them into
> these shapes.**

Which meaning of the word *buffet* is used in the sentence?

F. buf-fet (bə´ fet) *Verb*. to strike

G. buf-fet (bə´ fā) *Noun*. a side table

H. buf-fet (bə´ fā) *Noun*. an informal meal

I. buf-fet (bə´ fet) *Verb*. to struggle against

3 Read this sentence from the article.

> **Desert animals have special characteristics that
> allow them to adapt to the harsh settings.**

The word *settings* means

A. sand.

B. rocks.

C. woodlands.

D. surroundings.

4 Read this sentence from the article.

> **In hot deserts, some animals go on a quest for food early in the morning, the coolest time of the day.**

What does the word *quest* mean?

F. hike

G. search

H. promise

I. question

5 How are all deserts ALIKE?

A. They are very hot during the day.

B. They have many plants and animals.

C. They are sandy and get very little rainfall.

D. They have a harsh landscape with little rainfall.

6 How are the Sahara Desert and the Gobi Desert DIFFERENT?

F. The Sahara is cold all the time, but the Gobi is cold at night.

G. The Sahara is cold at night, but the Gobi is cold all the time.

H. The Sahara is hot during the day, but the Gobi is hot all the time.

I. The Sahara is cold during the day, but the Gobi is cold all the time.

© Macmillan/McGraw–Hill

Go On

7 According to the caption under the second illustration, what is the MOST LIKELY difference between a squirrel that lives in a neighborhood and an animal that lives in a desert?

    A. how fat they are

    B. how thick their fur is

    C. how fast they can run

    D. how well they can hide from enemies

8 How are lizards that live in a desert and bears that live in a forest ALIKE?

    F. They both like warm weather.

    G. They both hunt the same way.

    H. They both have trouble finding food in the winter.

    I. They both live off their fat when they cannot find food.

 Go On

9 Animals in hot deserts and animals in cold deserts do their hunting at different times of the day. Use information from the article to describe and explain these differences.

READ
THINK
EXPLAIN

_____

_____

_____

_____

_____

_____

_____

_____

_____

Go On ▶

Student Name _____

Read and answer questions 10–12 on your Answer Sheet.

10 Read this sentence.

> **The fishermen used metal <u>hooks</u> on <u>bambboo</u> rods to catch <u>tuna</u>, but they caught <u>few</u> fish.**

Which underlined word is spelled incorrectly?

- **A.** fcw
- **B.** tuna
- **C.** hooks
- **D.** bambboo

11 Read this sentence.

> **She had a good <u>veiw</u> of the <u>bruise</u>, which had a purple <u>hue</u> and looked like the <u>plume</u> of a feather.**

Which underlined word is spelled incorrectly?

- **F.** hue
- **G.** veiw
- **H.** plume
- **I.** bruise

12 Which word is spelled incorrectly?

- **A.** dutie
- **B.** brood
- **C.** prove
- **D.** amuse

Read the story "A Garden in the City." Choose the word or words that correctly complete questions 13–15.

A Garden in the City

Martin and his family had always lived in the country. Then his mother got a new job, (13) they had to move to a city. Martin liked his new (14) he really missed the big garden at his old house.

One day Martin walked by a big garden where people were working. He asked a man, "Is this your (15) do you just work here?"

The man told him that anyone in the neighborhood could have a garden there. Martin couldn't wait to tell his parents!

13 Which answer should go in blank (13)?

　F. or

　G. but

　H. and

14 Which answer should go in blank (14)?

　A. house but

　B. house but,

　C. house, but

15 Which answer should go in blank (15)?

　F. garden but

　G. garden, or

　H. garden, nor

Student Name _____

Grade 5 • Unit 1 • Week 3
Student Evaluation Chart

Tested Skills	Number Correct	Percent Correct
Vocabulary Strategies: *Homographs, 1, 2; synonyms, 3, 4*	/4	%
Reading Comprehension: *Compare and contrast, 5, 6, 7, 8*	/4	%
Short response: *Compare and contrast, 9*	/2	%
Spelling: *Words with /ü/, /ū/ and /ù/, 10, 11, 12*	/3	%
Grammar, Mechanics, and Usage: *Sentence combining, 13; punctuate compound sentences, 14, 15*	/3	%
Total Weekly Test Score	**/16**	**%**

Correlations

Item	FCAT Assessed Benchmarks*	New Sunshine State Standards
1	LA.A.1.2.3	LA.5.1.6.8
2	LA.A.1.2.3	LA.5.1.6.8
3	LA.A.1.2.3	LA.5.1.6.8
4	LA.A.1.2.3	LA.5.1.6.8
5	LA.A.2.2.7	LA.5.1.7.5
6	LA.A.2.2.7	LA.5.1.7.5
7	LA.A.2.2.7	LA.5.1.7.5
8	LA.A.2.2.7	LA.5.1.7.5
9	LA.A.2.2.7	LA.5.1.7.5
10		LA.5.1.7.5
11		LA.5.3.4.1
12		LA.5.3.4.1
13		LA.5.3.2.2
14		LA.5.3.4.3
15		LA.5.3.4.3

* See benchmarks and standards on pages 379–384.

© Macmillan/McGraw–Hill

Name _____

Date _____

FCAT Format Weekly Assessment

TESTED SKILLS AND STRATEGIES

- Vocabulary Strategies
- Reading Comprehension
- Spelling
- Grammar, Mechanics, and Usage

Macmillan
McGraw-Hill

Read the article "Exploring Space with Satellites" before answering Numbers 1 through 9.

Exploring Space with Satellites

People have always been interested in outer space. They have looked with wonder at the night sky. Long ago the Egyptians looked to the stars to predict floods. The early Greeks studied the Moon and stars to create a calendar.

Today we know much more about space. For more than 40 years, scientists have sent astronauts into space to explore. Astronauts get to space in rockets that break the grip of Earth's gravity. Gravity is the force that draws objects toward the center of Earth. It is a zone wrapped around Earth like a thick belt. Without gravity the environment on Earth would not be like it is today. Gravity makes Earth's air, water, plants, and animals possible.

Scientists do not just send people into space. They also send special machines, which are called satellites. Sometimes you can see satellites after dark. They move across the night sky and look like blinking lights.

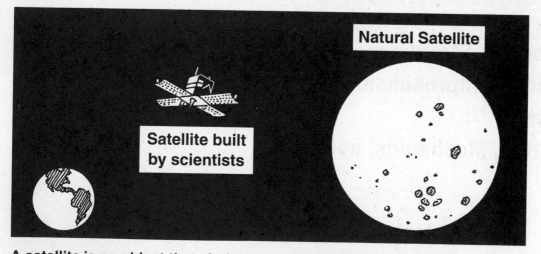

Natural Satellite

Satellite built by scientists

A satellite is an object that circles around another object. Some satellites, like the Moon, are natural. Other satellites are not natural. Scientists have built them.

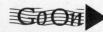

Some satellites explore space, just as astronauts do. They may study the Moon, the Sun, and stars. They may be sent to other planets. For example, a satellite took photos of Jupiter in 1979. These photos showed that Jupiter's great red spot is a huge storm. Other satellites explored Saturn's rings and moons. In 1997, a satellite was sent to Mars. It studied the planet's weather and land by taking photos. Some satellites study our own planet. They send information to computers. Some scientists use the information to study oceans. Others use it to make maps.

Not all satellites have the mission of exploring space. The job of some satellites is to carry signals over long distances. They carry TV, radio, and telephone signals. Some of the earliest satellites had this purpose. The first telephone and TV satellite went into space in 1962.

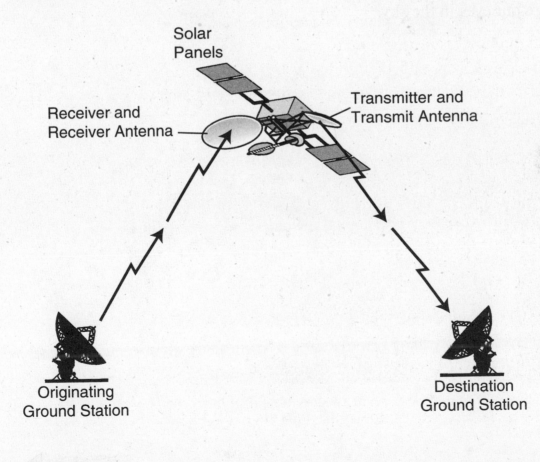

Go On ▶

Other satellites locate objects on Earth. They might locate ships, planes, or even cars. For this to happen, the object must have a special receiver.

Another kind of satellite studies weather. These satellites take photos of clouds and storms. They send this information to computers on Earth. The information helps scientists predict the weather. Weather satellites also were an early kind of satellite. The first one went into space in 1960.

Scientists work hard to avoid having problems with satellites. They plan for a long time. But disasters can happen. Some satellites get sucked into orbit. Others get lost in the maze of space. Others simply do not function. Sometimes these satellites are adjusted or replaced.

In spite of these problems, scientists keep sending satellites into space. They are our eyes in the sky.

Go On ▶

Student Name _____

Now answer Numbers 1 through 9 on your Answer Sheet. Base your answers on the article "Exploring Space with Satellites."

1 According to the article, what is *gravity*?

   A. a part of outer space

   B. the way that we can reach outer space

   C. the force that holds everything to Earth's surface

   D. a thick belt that forms a circle around the planets

2 Earth's *environment* includes all of the following EXCEPT

   F. air.

   G. water.

   H. plants.

   I. rockets.

3 Read these sentences from the article.

> **Not all satellites have the mission of exploring space. The job of some satellites is to carry signals over long distances.**

What clue in the sentences helps you define *mission*?

   A. job

   B. carry

   C. satellites

   D. exploring

Student Name _____

4 Read this sentence.

Other satellites simply do not function, or work, and have to be replaced with new ones.

Which word in the sentence helps you understand the meaning of *function*?

F. work

G. other

H. satellites

I. replaced

5 The main idea of this article is that

A. satellites perform several different functions.

B. satellites have been used for more than 40 years.

C. satellites send information to computers on Earth.

D. satellites sometimes have problems and must be replaced.

6 What is the MAIN idea of the first illustration and its caption?

F. Scientists build satellites.

G. The Moon is a natural satellite.

H. Some objects in the night sky circle around other objects.

I. Some satellites are natural, and some are built by scientists.

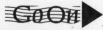

Student Name _____

7 What is the MAIN idea of the fourth paragraph of the article?

    A. Satellites have taken photos of some of the planets.

    B. Satellites usually are sent to other planets to study them.

    C. Satellites can take photos of a planet's weather and land.

    D. Satellites are used to explore Earth and other objects in space.

8 Which statement below BEST supports the idea that scientists work hard to avoid having problems with satellites?

    F. Scientists plan for a long time.

    G. Some satellites get lost in space.

    H. Some satellites have to be replaced.

    I. Some satellites get sucked into orbit.

GO On ▶

Student Name _____

9 What is the MAIN idea of the article? Use details and information from the article to explain how the author supports this idea.

READ
THINK
EXPLAIN

_____

_____

_____

_____

_____

_____

_____

_____

_____

_____

_____

_____

_____

_____

_____

Go On

Student Name _____

Read and answer questions 10–12 on your Answer Sheet.

10 Read this sentence.

The <u>harsh</u> bushes and the <u>corse</u> weeds on the path to the <u>marsh</u> made us change our <u>course</u>.

Which underlined word is spelled incorrectly?

A. corse

B. harsh

C. marsh

D. course

11 Which word is spelled incorrectly?

F. barge

G. sqares

H. scarce

I. source

12 Read this sentence.

With <u>scorne</u> for his enemy, the pirate <u>swore</u> revenge as he waved his <u>sword</u> with tremendous <u>force</u>.

Which underlined word is spelled incorrectly?

A. force

B. swore

C. sword

D. scorne

Go On ▶

Student Name _____

Read and answer questions 13–15 on your Answer Sheet.

 Which sentence below is a **complex sentence**?

    F. The auditorium is crowded because the play is popular.

    G. The actors are in their costumes, and they are ready to begin.

    H. The drama teacher is about to go on stage and talk to the audience.

14 Combine the ideas in the box to create a logical sentence.

> **Keira called Marta**
>
> **Nobody answered**

Which sentence below correctly combines the ideas in the box?

    A. Keira called Marta, nobody answered.

    B. Keira called Marta if nobody answered.

    C. Keira called Marta, but nobody answered.

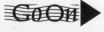

15 Read the letter in the box.

> **Dear Director Alford:**
>
> **Please remove me from your list of subscribers. I no longer wish to receive the *Evansdale Gazette*. Thank you for your cooperation.**
>
> > **sincerely yours**
> >
> > **Adam Remoth**

In which closing below are all **punctuation** and **capitalization** correct?

F. Sincerely yours

G. Sincerely yours,

H. Sincerely, yours

STOP

Student Name _____

Grade 5 • Unit 1 • Week 4
Student Evaluation Chart

Tested Skills	Number Correct	Percent Correct
Vocabulary Strategies: *Context clues: look for a description or explanation,* 1, 2, 3, 4	/4	%
Reading Comprehension: *Main idea and details,* 5, 6, 7, 8	/4	%
Extended response: *Main idea and details,* 9	/4	%
Spelling: *Words with /är/, /âr/, and /ôr/,* 10, 11, 12	/3	%
Grammar, Mechanics, and Usage: *More sentence combining/complex sentences,* 13, 14; *use commas and capital letters in a letter,* 15	/3	%
Total Weekly Test Score	**/18**	%

Correlations

Item	FCAT Assessed Benchmarks*	New Sunshine State Standards
1	LA.A.1.2.3	LA.5.1.6.3
2	LA.A.1.2.3	LA.5.1.6.3
3	LA.A.1.2.3	LA.5.1.6.3
4	LA.A.1.2.3	LA.5.1.6.3
5	LA.A.2.2.1	LA.5.2.2.2
6	LA.A.2.2.1	LA.5.2.2.2
7	LA.A.2.2.1	LA.5.2.2.2
8	LA.A.2.2.1	LA.5.2.2.2
9	LA.A.2.2.1	LA.5.2.2.2
10		LA.5.3.4.1
11		LA.5.3.4.1
12		LA.5.3.4.1
13		LA.5.3.2.2
14		LA.5.3.2.2
15		LA.5.3.4.3

* See benchmarks and standards on pages 379–384.

Name _____

Date _____

FCAT Format Weekly Assessment

TESTED SKILLS AND STRATEGIES

- **Vocabulary Strategies**
- **Reading Comprehension**
- **Spelling**
- **Grammar, Mechanics, and Usage**

Macmillan McGraw-Hill

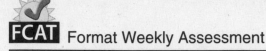
Read the story "A Surprising Ski Trip" before answering Numbers 1 through 9.

A Surprising Ski Trip

"Are you almost ready to go?" Ellen asked her brother Ben. They were in back of their house, which was located in the mountains.

Ben moistened a finger by sticking it in the wet snow and then held it up in the air. "The wind is coming from the north, and that means it's about to snow again. Besides, it's too warm to ski." He hesitated, then said, "I really don't think we should ski today. The conditions aren't right."

Ellen put her hands on her hips, frowned, and said, "You always have a ridiculous theory that spoils my fun. Last week the snow wasn't dry enough. This time it's the wind and weather." She raised her voice a little higher. "Ben, today is my birthday, and in celebration of my birthday I want to go skiing. You canceled our ski trip last week. So today we're going skiing."

Ben was worried. He pulled his ski hat down over his ears and took off walking. Ellen followed close behind him.

© Macmillan/McGraw-Hill

Go On ▶

The cold wind made the kids' cheeks glow. They enjoyed the crisp air and the quiet. "I feel like we're alone in the world! And it's a wonderful feeling!" Ellen yelled. Ben agreed, but he didn't feel so comfortable about it.

Suddenly Ben heard a low roar, like a lion in the distance. "What is that? What could cause that kind of noise?" he wondered to himself.

The sound was getting closer—and quickly! With a sickening thud in his stomach, Ben realized the noise must be the result of an avalanche! Before he could warn Ellen, the wall of snow swallowed them up, and Ben and Ellen were trapped under the snow.

A half mile away, ski patrolman Eric Camacho listened to the avalanche call on his radio. "Two skiers are trapped," said the voice on the radio.

Eric and his rescue dog Mars raced to the place that had been described. All around them, everything was blanketed in white. The snow was deep, but Mars immediately started digging. In just a few minutes, the animal found Ben and Ellen. They were scared and slightly bruised, but neither one had any serious injuries.

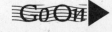

Eric called for assistance, and then he calmed the two kids. "You were fortunate. Mars is a well-trained dog with a good nose, and he found you quickly," he said.

Ellen said, her voice shaking a little, "I'm glad I wore perfume. It's a new fragrance. I'm sure Mars smelled it."

"Mars would have found you even without that smell," the patrolman said. "Our rescue dogs have a variety of ways to find lost skiers. It's not easy to find people when the landscape has been transformed by an avalanche. That's why our rescue dogs are so important."

On their way home, both Ellen and Ben reached an agreement. They decided that they would carefully consider many things before going on another ski trip.

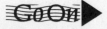

Student Name _____

Now answer Numbers 1 through 9 on your Answer Sheet.
Base your answers on the story "A Surprising Ski Trip."

1 Read this sentence from the story.

Ben moistened a finger by sticking it in the wet snow and then held it up in the air.

Which word means almost the SAME as the word *moistened*?

A. bent

B. froze

C. wetted

D. pointed

2 Read these sentences from the story.

"I'm glad I wore perfume. It's a new fragrance."

Which word means almost the SAME as the word *fragrance*?

F. feel

G. sight

H. taste

I. smell

3 Read this sentence.

The birthday celebration lasted long into the night.

The word *celebration* means

A. cake.

B. song.

C. party.

D. presents.

© Macmillan/McGraw–Hill

Go On ▶

Read the thesaurus entry.

theory–*Noun.* guess, _____, hypothesis

Which synonym belongs in the blank in the thesaurus entry?

F. fact

G. truth

H. variety

I. explanation

5 What causes Ben to worry in the beginning of the story?

A. He is not a good skier.

B. His sister does not know how to ski.

C. He often gets hurt when he goes skiing.

D. He thinks the weather is not good for skiing.

6 Why does Ellen feel so strongly about wanting to ski on this exact day?

F. It is Ellen's birthday.

G. Ben canceled their last ski trip.

H. Ellen thinks the weather is perfect for skiing.

I. Ellen wants to feel like she is alone in the world.

7 The strange noise that Ben hears is caused by

    A. the roar of a lion.

    B. an avalanche of snow.

    C. the strong wind howling.

    D. the barking of a rescue dog.

8 Which statement below is NOT an effect of the avalanche?

    F. Ben and Ellen are badly hurt.

    G. Ben and Ellen are buried in snow.

    H. Eric and Mars look for Ben and Ellen.

    I. Eric hears about Ben and Ellen on his radio.

Go On ▶

9 What effect might their experience with the avalanche have on Ellen and Ben? Use details and information from the story to support your answer.

READ
THINK
EXPLAIN

_____

_____

_____

_____

_____

_____

_____

_____

_____

© Macmillan/McGraw–Hill

GoOn ▶

Read and answer questions 10–12 on your Answer Sheet.

10 Read this sentence.

> Since it is a <u>dreary</u> day, Maritza <u>yerns</u> for <u>clear</u>, blue skies and a sprinkler that <u>spurts</u> water all over the garden.

Which underlined word is spelled incorrectly?

A. clear

B. yerns

C. dreary

D. spurts

11 Read this sentence.

> Every <u>year</u> the family goes to the beach to play in the <u>surf</u>, <u>squirt</u> water at each other, and watch the crabs <u>sqirm</u>.

Which underlined word is spelled incorrectly?

F. year

G. surf

H. sqirm

I. squirt

12 Which word is spelled incorrectly?

A. lurk

B. lurch

C. verse

D. therst

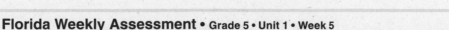

Student Name _____

The article below is a first draft. The article contains errors. Read the article to answer questions 13 and 14.

→ 1 People around the world love the Olympic Games. 2 One symbol of the Games. 3 The flame comes from Olympia, Greece, where the first Games were held. 4 According to custom, the Olympic flame must be lit by the sun. 5 Relay runners carry the flame from Greece to the city where the games will be held, the flame stands for knowledge, spirit, and life. 6 Passing the flame shows how the traditions of the Olympics continue from generation to generation.

What do these mean?

1 This type of symbol is in the Florida test to show a sentence number.

→ This symbol in the test shows a new paragraph.

The test may include the kinds of writing you might do. You will be asked to change and improve the writing.

Go On ▶

13 Which sentence is a NOT a complete sentence?

F. sentence $\boxed{1}$ H. sentence $\boxed{3}$

G. sentence $\boxed{2}$ I. sentence $\boxed{4}$

14 Which sentence is a **run-on sentence**?

A. sentence $\boxed{3}$ C. sentence $\boxed{5}$

B. sentence $\boxed{4}$ D. sentence $\boxed{6}$

Read and answer question 15 on your Answer Sheet.

15 Read the sentence in the box.

> **LaShonda spent the morning skateboarding many people watched her.**

What is the BEST way to correct the sentence in the box?

F. LaShonda spent the morning skateboarding, many people watched her.

G. LaShonda spent the morning skateboarding, or many people watched her.

H. LaShonda spent the morning skateboarding, and many people watched her.

Student Name _____

Student Evaluation Chart

Tested Skills	Number Correct	Percent Correct
Vocabulary Strategies: *Synonyms*, 1, 2, 3, 4	/4	%
Reading Comprehension: *Cause and effect*, 5, 6, 7, 8	/4	%
Short response: *Cause and effect*, 9	/2	%
Spelling: *Words with /ûr/ and /îr/*, 10, 11, 12	/3	%
Grammar, Mechanics, and Usage: *Sentence fragments*, 13; *run-on sentences*, 14, 15	/3	%

	Number Correct	Percent Correct
Total Weekly Test Score	/16	%

Correlations

Item	FCAT Assessed Benchmarks*	New Sunshine State Standards
1	LA.A.1.2.3	LA.5.1.6.8
2	LA.A.1.2.3	LA.5.1.6.8
3	LA.A.1.2.3	LA.5.1.6.8
4	LA.A.1.2.3	LA.5.1.6.8
5	LA.E.2.2.1	LA.5.1.7.4
6	LA.E.2.2.1	LA.5.1.7.4
7	LA.E.2.2.1	LA.5.1.7.4
8	LA.E.2.2.1	LA.5.1.7.4
9	LA.E.2.2.1	LA.5.1.7.4
10		LA.5.3.4.1
11		LA.5.3.4.1
12		LA.5.3.4.1
13		LA.5.3.2.2
14		LA.5.3.2.2
15		LA.5.3.2.2

* See benchmarks and standards on pages 379–384.

FLORIDA
Treasures

Name _____

Date _____

FCAT Format
Weekly
Assessment

TESTED SKILLS AND STRATEGIES

- Vocabulary Strategies
- Reading Comprehension
- Spelling
- Grammar, Mechanics, and Usage

Macmillan
McGraw-Hill

Read the story "Something to Do" before answering Numbers 1 through 9.

Something to Do

Kyle needed something better to do with his time. He had been spending summer afternoons watching TV and slurping soda. His dad would warn him to turn off the TV set now and then. Each time Kyle would protest, and his dad would reply, "I'd have more sympathy for you if you worked as hard as I do!"

Kyle decided to get a job. Unfortunately everyone said he was too young for a "real" job. One afternoon Kyle lingered in the lobby of his apartment building, feeling mournful. Mr. Jackson, the custodian for the building, stopped to chat and find out what was wrong. At first Kyle didn't want to admit how bored he was. But he considered Mr. Jackson a friend, and finally he told him.

© Macmillan/McGraw-Hill

Go On ▶

The custodian thought about Kyle's problem for a moment. "Well," he began, "several elderly residents in this building can't get outside much anymore. Maybe you could run errands for them."

"That's a great idea!" exclaimed Kyle.

Later that afternoon Kyle posted a flyer on the bulletin board in the lobby. Days went by, and he didn't receive a single phone call in response to the flyer. He found this bewildering. In the flyer he had named really low prices for his services.

He left his apartment in search of Mr. Jackson. The custodian was delivering a package to a resident. Kyle told him about not getting any phone calls.

"That's strange," Mr. Jackson told Kyle. "I know that Mrs. Kim's dog needs exercise, but she can't walk him. And Mr. Castelli has an injury and needs someone to pick up his prescriptions. Maybe they just don't have money to spare."

Kyle could hardly believe his ears. He simply couldn't associate his building's luxurious apartments and fancy lobby with people who were struggling to make ends meet. Mr. Jackson must have read his mind. He said, "Some of the residents have lived in this building a long time. It's hard to pay rent that keeps going up when your income stays the same."

Kyle hesitated then said, "You know, I'm mainly looking for something to keep me busy until school starts. The pay isn't the main consideration for me."

Go On ▶

"It is for them, Kyle," Mr. Jackson said.

Kyle understood what he meant. He rode the elevator to the third floor, walked down the hall, and knocked on a door. Mrs. Kim opened it. But before she could say anything Kyle asked, "Would you like me to walk your dog? There's no charge."

A little dog peeked at Kyle from around the door. "Oh, what decency!" said Mrs. Kim. "Trixie is a little shy, but she'll take to you quickly. And maybe in the future I can find a way to return the favor."

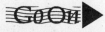

Student Name _____

Now answer Numbers 1 through 9 on your Answer Sheet.
Base your answers on the story "Something to Do."

1 Read this sentence from the story.

> **"I'd have more sympathy for you if you worked as hard as I do!"**

Which word could replace *sympathy* In the sentence?

A. time

B. respect

C. interest

D. understanding

2 Read this sentence from the story.

> **One afternoon Kyle lingered in the lobby of his apartment building, feeling mournful.**

Which word means almost the SAME as *mournful*?

F. unhappy

G. confused

H. badly treated

I. misunderstood

3 Read this sentence from the story.

> **He simply couldn't associate his building's luxurious apartments and fancy lobby with people who were struggling to make ends meet.**

What does the author mean by *make ends meet*?

A. come to the end of

B. make a connection

C. arrive at an agreement with

D. have enough money for expenses

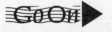

4 Read this sentence from the story.

Mr. Jackson must have read his mind.

What does the idiom *read his mind* mean?

F. thought in a similar way to Kyle

G. guessed what Kyle was thinking

H. believed that Kyle had a good mind

I. thought Kyle could read to avoid being bored

5 In the story, Mrs. Kim says that Trixie, her dog, will take to Kyle quickly.

What does the idiom *take to* mean?

A. get used to

B. look shyly at

C. run away from

D. be patient with

6 You can tell from the story that Kyle's father

F. often is cruel and unfair to Kyle.

G. never takes time out to have fun.

H. wants Kyle to use his time wisely.

I. wants to get rid of the television set.

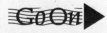

© Macmillan/McGraw–Hill

7 Mr. Jackson is someone who

   A. is too busy to think of others.

   B. wants to help all young people.

   C. understands how to help people.

   D. does not believe Kyle is very responsible.

8 How will Kyle MOST LIKELY spend the rest of his summer afternoons?

   F. playing with Mrs. Kim's little dog

   G. sitting in front of the television set

   H. helping out the elderly people in his building

   I. working at his father's office as an errand boy

Go On ▶

9 How does Mr. Jackson influence Kyle? What does Kyle learn from Mr. Jackson? Use details and information from the story in your answer.

READ
THINK
EXPLAIN

_____

_____

_____

_____

_____

_____

_____

_____

_____

GoOn ▶

Student Name _____

Read and answer questions 10–12 on your Answer Sheet.

10 Which word or group of words is spelled incorrectly?

    A. all right

    B. armchair

    C. pillocase

    D. overcome

11 Read this sentence.

    We spent the <u>after noon</u> in the <u>cornfield</u>, watching an <u>earthworm</u> play with a piece of <u>cardboard</u>.

Which underlined word or group of words is spelled incorrectly?

    F. cornfield

    G. after noon

    H. cardboard

    I. earthworm

12 Read this sentence.

    On the <u>field trip</u>, <u>ninetyone</u> people went <u>ice-skating</u>, including the president and <u>vice president</u> of the fifth-grade class.

Which underlined word or group of words is spelled incorrectly?

    A. field trip

    B. ninetyone

    C. ice-skating

    D. vice president

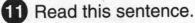

Student Name _____

Read the story "Holidays." Choose the word or words that correctly complete questions 13 and 14.

Holidays

You'll see many, many holidays named on any calendar used in the United States. Some of them are celebrated for religious reasons, and others are celebrated for historical reasons.

Probably the most important historical holiday is the (13). On this day, Americans celebrate the declaration of our country's independence from England.

(14) is another historical holiday. On this day, Americans remember the Pilgrims' first harvest. It is celebrated on the fourth Thursday in November.

13 Which answer should go in blank (13)?

F. Fourth of july

G. fourth of July

H. Fourth of July

14 Which answer should go in blank (14)?

A. Thanksgiving

B. Thanks giving

C. Thanks Giving

GoOn ▶

Read and answer question 15 on your Answer Sheet.

15 In which sentence below is all **capitalization** correct?

    F. Is Oklahoma city the capital of Oklahoma?

    G. The state park is northwest of Sand Hill Lake.

    H. Shaundra likes to wear a costume on her Birthday.

STOP

Student Name _____

Grade 5 • Unit 2 • Week 1
Student Evaluation Chart

Tested Skills	Number Correct	Percent Correct
Vocabulary Strategies: *Synonyms*, 1, 2; *idioms*, 3, 4, 5	/5	%
Reading Comprehension: *Plot development: make inferences*, 6, 7, 8	/3	%
Short response: *Plot development: make inferences*, 9	/2	%
Spelling: *Compound words*, 10, 11, 12	/3	%
Grammar, Mechanics, and Usage: *Common and proper nouns*, 13, 14, 15	/3	%
Total Weekly Test Score	**/16**	**%**

Correlations

Item	FCAT Assessed Benchmarks*	New Sunshine State Standards
1	LA.A.1.2.3	LA.5.1.6.8
2	LA.A.1.2.3	LA.5.1.6.8
3	LA.A.1.2.3	LA.5.1.6.9
4	LA.A.1.2.3	LA.5.1.6.9
5	LA.A.1.2.3	LA.5.1.6.9
6	LA.E.1.2.2	LA.5.2.1.2
7	LA.E.1.2.2	LA.5.2.1.2
8	LA.E.1.2.2	LA.5.2.1.2
9	LA.E.1.2.2	LA.5.2.1.2
10		LA.5.3.4.1
11		LA.5.3.4.1
12		LA.5.3.4.1
13		LA.5.3.4.2
14		LA.5.3.4.2
15		LA.5.3.4.2

* See benchmarks and standards on pages 379–384.

Name _____

Date _____

FCAT Format Weekly Assessment

TESTED SKILLS AND STRATEGIES

- Vocabulary Strategies
- Reading Comprehension
- Spelling
- Grammar, Mechanics, and Usage

Macmillan McGraw-Hill

**Read the article "Super Snakes" before answering
Numbers 1 through 9.**

Super Snakes

Many people fear snakes because they know only the common myths about this reptile. Few snakes are deadly. However, poisonous species have certainly given snakes a bad reputation! Here are some facts about the snake that will help you to better understand this member of the animal kingdom.

Snakes can survive in many surroundings, except for the polar regions of the world. Nature has given this creature many gifts. One of these is the way its skin looks. Its patterns or coloring, or both, help the reptile to hide from predators that would attack and eat it.

Many species of snake have skin the dull color of earth. The kinds that slither up trees may be bright green, like leaves.

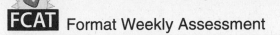
Snakes can go for weeks or even months between meals, and some snakes eat only once or twice a year. Because of this, they do not need to hunt constantly for food.

The lunging and flickering tongue of the snake may look frightening as it vibrates. But the tongue is part of an important sense organ for the snake. There is a special organ on the roof of its mouth. The snake uses it to smell prey and to find a mate. Some snakes, like the python, have special cells on top of their heads. These cells help them to locate warm-blooded animals.

Snakes use the muscles along the sides of their bodies to slither from place to place.

Most snakes feed on small animals like rats and mice. Big snakes, like pythons, will attack much larger prey. Alert and watchful, the snake will often win what look like impossible battles.

The snake slithers on its belly because it has no legs. To move, it tightens and then relaxes the muscles along the sides of its body. It also can use its tail to push off against rocks or other objects. Because it can move so rapidly and quietly, the snake is a very effective hunter.

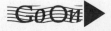

It is true that some snakes are poisonous. They use their poison to stun their prey before eating it. It always is best to be careful around snakes. Only an expert can tell which snakes are harmless and which are dangerous.

However, a person can be careful around snakes without having a fear of them. The best advice is to find out if any poisonous snakes live in your area. In addition, if you are going camping or hiking, check beforehand to find out if the area is a habitat for poisonous snakes. If any poisonous snakes are found where you live or will be visiting, learn to identify them. Also learn what steps to take when you come across a poisonous snake. With knowledge like this, you can replace your fear with caution.

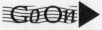

Student Name _____

**Now answer Numbers 1 through 9 on your Answer Sheet.
Base your answers on the article "Super Snakes."**

1 Read this sentence from the article.

> **Its patterns and coloring, or both, help the reptile
> to hide from predators that would attack and eat it.**

According to the sentence, what do *predators* do?

A. help other animals

B. avoid other animals

C. hunt other animals as food

D. live in the branches of trees

2 Read this sentence from the article.

> **Alert and watchful, the snake will often win what
> look like impossible battles.**

Which word means almost the SAME as *alert*?

F. safe

G. quick

H. aware

I. dangerous

3 Read this sentence.

> **Snakes can survive in many surroundings.**

Which word could replace *surroundings*?

A. prey

B. earth

C. settings

D. temperatures

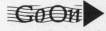

© Macmillan/McGraw–Hill

4 Read this sentence from the article.

Many species of snake have skin the dull color of earth.

Which word means almost the SAME as *species*?

F. kinds

G. babies

H. patterns

I. members

5 What is the MAIN idea of the second paragraph?

A. Snakes cannot live in the polar regions of the world.

B. Snakes have been given special and unusual gifts by nature.

C. Snakes have features that allow them to live in many places.

D. A snake's skin may have an unusual pattern or coloring, or both.

6 The caption under the first illustration is MAINLY about

F. the way snakes look.

G. the way snakes move.

H. why snakes are bright green.

I. when snakes are most likely to move.

© Macmillan/McGraw–Hill

7 Which sentence BEST tells what the fourth paragraph is about?

    A. The snake has a strange way of finding a mate.

    B. The snake does not use its nose to smell things.

    C. The snake's flickering tongue often scares people.

    D. The snake's tongue is part of an important sense organ.

8 According to the author of the article,

    F. some snakes poison their prey before eating it.

    G. the scales on many snakes' bodies help them move.

    H. some snakes can travel at speeds of up to six miles an hour.

    I. the sense of smell is more important than eyesight for most snakes.

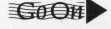

9 The author of "Super Snakes" provides readers with many facts. Use information from the article to explain:

READ
THINK
EXPLAIN

- the MAIN idea of the article, and
- how the details of the article support the main idea

_____

_____

_____

_____

_____

_____

_____

_____

_____

_____

_____

_____

_____

_____

_____

_____

_____

_____

_____

© Macmillan/McGraw–Hill

Go On ▶

Student Name _____

Read and answer question 10–12 on your Answer Sheet.

10 Read this sentence.

> All the <u>countries</u> sent <u>batchs</u> of <u>potatoes</u> to pay their <u>taxes</u>.

Which underlined word is spelled incorrectly?

A. taxes

B. batchs

C. potatoes

D. countries

11 Which word is spelled incorrectly?

F. lashes

G. notches

H. beliefes

I. liberties

12 Read this sentence.

> The <u>rattlers</u> posed <u>difficultys</u>, and the owners of the <u>rodeos</u> knew they faced serious <u>losses</u>.

Which underlined word is spelled incorrectly?

A. losses

B. rodeos

C. rattlers

D. difficultys

© Macmillan/McGraw-Hill

GoOn ▶

Student Name _____

Read the letter. Choose the word or words that correctly complete questions 13 and 14.

Dear Sir or (13)

I have been ordering products from your company for five years. Until now I have always been satisfied with your products and service. However, I am writing you now with a complaint.

Last month I ordered two (14) of pale blue stationery and a package of matching envelopes. First, it took three weeks for my order to arrive. Second, some of the pages of stationery were cut crooked. Third, the envelopes were dark yellow.

Enclosed you will find your stationery and envelopes. Please return my money as soon as possible.

Sincerely,

Mary Elizabeth Henderson

13 Which answer should go in blank (13)?

F. Madam,

G. Madam:

H. Madam—

14 Which answer should go in blank (14)?

A. boxs

B. boxes

C. boxes'

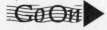

Read and answer question 15 on your Answer Sheet.

15 In which sentence below are all **plural nouns** correct?

   F. Many farmers in this region grow tomatoes.

   G. Their enemys are the insects that eat their crops.

   H. Some insects eat the leafs, while others destroy the fruit.

Grade 5 · Unit 2 · Week 2
Student Evaluation Chart

Tested Skills	Number Correct	Percent Correct
Vocabulary Strategies: *Synonyms*, 1, 4; *context clues: look for restatement*, 2, 3	/4	%
Reading Comprehension: *Main idea and details*, 5, 6, 7, 8	/4	%
Extended response: *Main idea and details*, 9	/4	%
Spelling: *Plural endings*, 10, 11, 12	/3	%
Grammar, Mechanics, and Usage: *Punctuating a formal letter*, 13; *singular and plural nouns*, 14, 15	/3	%
Total Weekly Test Score	/18	%

Correlations

Item	FCAT Assessed Benchmarks*	New Sunshine State Standards
1	LA.A.1.2.3	LA.5.1.6.8
2	LA.A.1.2.3	LA.5.1.6.3
3	LA.A.1.2.3	LA.5.1.6.3
4	LA.A.1.2.3	LA.5.1.6.8
5	LA.A.2.2.1	LA.5.1.7.3
6	LA.A.2.2.1	LA.5.1.7.3
7	LA.A.2.2.1	LA.5.1.7.3
8	LA.A.2.2.1	LA.5.1.7.3
9	LA.A.2.2.1	LA.5.1.7.3
10		LA.5.3.4.1
11		LA.5.3.4.1
12		LA.5.3.4.1
13		LA.5.3.4.3
14		LA.5.3.4.4
15		LA.5.3.4.4

* See benchmarks and standards on pages 379–384.

Name _____

Date _____

FCAT Format Weekly Assessment

TESTED SKILLS AND STRATEGIES

- **Vocabulary Strategies**
- **Reading Comprehension**
- **Spelling**
- **Grammar, Mechanics, and Usage**

Macmillan McGraw-Hill

Read the article "Life in the Middle Ages" before answering Numbers 1 through 9.

Life in the Middle Ages

The Middle Ages began more than 1,000 years ago and lasted about 500 years. This period is called the Middle Ages because it occurred between ancient and modern times.

The upper class owned the land, but the lower class worked it.

People in the Middle Ages lived in a social system in which there were strict divisions between social classes. Each social class was based on the kinds of jobs people held and their level of wealth. Because there was no equality in this system, people from different social classes were treated in very different ways. The kings and queens were the most powerful people. They owned most of the land and were considered the upper class. The people who worked for the church were almost as powerful as the royalty. Then came the professionals, such as doctors, lawyers, bankers, merchants, and skilled trades people, who made up the middle class.

© Macmillan/McGraw–Hill

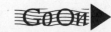

The farmers who worked the land were very poor and had very little power. They made up the lower class. They did not own their land or their homes, and they worked for the landowners. In turn, the landowners usually gave them protection from thieves and invading armies.

Education in the Middle Ages was mainly for young people from wealthy families. Of the girls who were educated, most studied in their own homes or in the homes of other wealthy families. Most of them learned the skills needed to manage a household, and some also learned to sing or play musical instruments. Most boys went to schools run by the church. Boys did not study what you study today. Back then, they learned only reading, writing, and some math. Most of the young people who got an education planned to enter religious life.

There also was a different kind of education in the Middle Ages. Between the ages of seven and twelve, some children learned by working with people who had already mastered trades or crafts. The students worked in stores or workshops with the masters.

Some young people dedicated seven years to learning a trade or craft. At the end of that time, they could open their own workshops or stores.

The number of young people who studied or learned a trade or craft was small, however. Most children did not get an education at all. They went right to work at an early age.

How do we know so much about the Middle Ages? Historians learn about the past from several sources. They read the writings of people who lived during a certain period. They carefully examine paintings, drawings, and other types of art created during the period. They also learn about the past from artifacts. These are objects made by people at some point in history. Artifacts might be tools, household items, or clothing. Often the artifacts are found at the site where they were used, such as a home, church, or workshop. Many of these items are now in museum exhibits.

GoOn ▶

Student Name _____

Now answer Numbers 1 through 9 on your Answer Sheet. Base your answers on the article "Life in the Middle Ages."

1 Read this sentence from the article.

> **Because there was no equality in this system, people from different social classes were treated in very different ways.**

What does the word *equality* mean?

A. matching each other

B. having the same rights

C. adding the same amount

D. having the same experiences

2 Read this sentence from the article.

> **Some young people dedicated seven years to learning a trade or craft.**

What does the word *dedicated* mean?

F. already devoted time

G. are devoting time now

H. have not yet devoted time

I. will devote time in the future

3 Which word below indicates that there is more than one?

A. goes

B. finds

C. learns

D. exhibits

Go On ▶

4 Read this sentence.

> **The object was placed in the museum with the other artifacts made by people long ago.**

Which items below could be the *artifacts* mentioned in the sentence?

F. seashells

G. cooking pots

H. animal bones

I. rocks in a riverbed

5 The MAIN idea of this article is that

A. farmers in the Middle Ages were very poor.

B. the Middle Ages took place a long time ago.

C. life in the Middle Ages was quite different from the present.

D. the Middle Ages can be studied through artifacts of that period.

6 What is the MAIN idea of the second paragraph?

F. People belonged to social classes.

G. Religious people had a lot of power.

H. Farmers were poor and did not own land.

I. Kings and queens owned most of the land.

7 For which topic does the caption under the second illustration give the MOST support?

   A. Education in the Middle Ages

   B. Studying Artifacts from the Middle Ages

   C. The Power of Social Classes in the Middle Ages

   D. Differences in Girls' and Boys' Education in the Middle Ages

8 Why did farmers have very little power during the Middle Ages?

   F. Most children went to work in the fields at an early age.

   G. Social class was based on the work people did and on their wealth.

   H. Between the ages of seven and twelve, some children learned trades or crafts.

   I. Landowners usually gave farmers protection from thieves and invading armies.

Go On ▶

9 How does the author help the reader to understand what life was like in the Middle Ages? Use information and details from the article to support your answer.

READ
THINK
EXPLAIN

_____

_____

_____

_____

_____

_____

_____

_____

_____

_____

_____

_____

_____

_____

_____

_____

_____

GoOn ▶

Student Name _____

Read and answer questions 10–12 on your Answer Sheet.

10 Read this sentence.

> **Because they were <u>fasinated</u> by the <u>complicated</u> and <u>amusing</u> puzzle, the children <u>regretted</u> having to go to bed.**

Which underlined word is spelled incorrectly?

A. amusing

B. regretted

C. fasinated

D. complicated

11 Which word is spelled incorrectly?

F. relied

G. applied

H. reffered

I. forbidding

12 Read this sentence.

> **People can get <u>injired</u> while <u>jogging</u> through the woods, especially if rain is <u>dripping</u> from the <u>gnarled</u> trees on the paths.**

Which underlined word is spelled incorrectly?

A. injired

B. jogging

C. gnarled

D. dripping

Go On ▶

Read and answer questions 13–15 on your Answer Sheet.

13 Which sentence below contains an error?

    F. The farmer had geese and turkies.

    G. The sheep are grazing on the lawn.

    H. Tomatoes are growing on the patios.

14 Read the sentence in the box.

> **During the holidays, the familys are getting together; right now all the husbands, wives, and children are decorating the rooms.**

What is the BEST way to correct the sentence in the box?

    A. Change *wives* to *wifes*.

    B. Change *familys* to *families*.

    C. Change *children* to *childrens*.

Student Name _____

15 In which sentence below are all **plural nouns** correct?

    F. The gardeneres have not worked in the garden for two weeks.

    G. The bushs need trimming, and there are many insects on the plants.

    H. The apples and peaches need to be picked, and tree branches need to be cut.

STOP

Student Name _____

Student Evaluation Chart

Tested Skills	Number Correct	Percent Correct
Vocabulary Strategies: *Context clues, 1, 4; inflectional endings, 2, 3*	/4	%
Reading Comprehension: *Main idea and details, 5, 6, 7, 8*	/4	%
Extended response: *Main idea and details, 9*	/4	%
Spelling: *Inflectional endings, 10, 11, 12*	/3	%
Grammar, Mechanics, and Usage: *More plural nouns, 13, 14, 15*	/3	%

Total Weekly Test Score	/18	%

Correlations

Item	FCAT Assessed Benchmarks*	New Sunshine State Standards
1	LA.A.1.2.3	LA.5.1.6.3
2	LA.A.1.2.3	LA.5.1.6.7
3	LA.A.1.2.3	LA.5.1.6.7
4	LA.A.1.2.3	LA.5.1.6.3
5	LA.A.2.2.1	LA.5.1.7.3
6	LA.A.2.2.1	LA.5.1.7.3
7	LA.A.2.2.1	LA.5.1.7.3
8	LA.A.2.2.1	LA.5.1.7.3
9	LA.A.2.2.1	LA.5.1.7.3
10		LA.5.3.4.1
11		LA.5.3.4.1
12		LA.5.3.4.1
13		LA.5.3.4.4
14		LA.5.3.4.4
15		LA.5.3.4.4

* See benchmarks and standards on pages 379–384.

FLORIDA
Treasures

Name _____

Date _____

FCAT Format Weekly Assessment

TESTED SKILLS AND STRATEGIES

- **Vocabulary Strategies**
- **Reading Comprehension**
- **Spelling**
- **Grammar, Mechanics, and Usage**

Macmillan
McGraw-Hill

Read the story "A Carnival Costume" before answering Numbers 1 through 9.

A Carnival Costume

Marisol lived on the Caribbean island of Trinidad. Carnival was approaching. It was a celebration filled with parades, dances, and music, and almost everyone on the island would join the fun. But Marisol had a problem: How could she get a costume for it?

"Carnival is so special," she said to her friend Nicolette one day. "I really want to wear a beautiful costume that everyone will notice."

"Do you want an elegant, fancy costume?" Nicolette asked.

"Well, that would be irresistible. Who could turn that down?" Marisol said slowly, with hesitation. "But I'm reluctant to ask my parents because a fancy costume costs a lot of money."

"Why don't we make you a costume?" Nicolette suggested.

"We don't know how to sew," Marisol replied.

"That won't be a problem," Nicolette assured her. The girls went to Marisol's house and sewed fabric scraps together. As they worked, they gossiped about the people in their neighborhood. They shared rumors they had heard about everyone.

When the costume was finished, Marisol tried it on. "It's ugly," she said. "And it doesn't fit me right."

"You're right. It's horrible," Nicolette agreed. "What can we do now?"

"Let's ask your grandmother to help us," Marisol said. "She makes beautiful costumes." But the girls knew that Mrs. Blanco would be very busy making costumes for Carnival.

Nicolette and Marisol walked to Mrs. Blanco's store. It was filled with customers. Throwing feathers into the air, mischievous kids ran in and out of the racks of brightly colored skirts and tops. The kids' mothers told them, "You must stop. Running like that is forbidden in Mrs. Blanco's store." But the kids giggled and continued to run.

Nicolette explained Marisol's problem to her grandmother. Mrs. Blanco said, "I'd like to help you, Marisol. But I have too much work to do. This is my busiest season of the year."

"Grandmother, what if we help you by cleaning the store?" Nicolette asked.

"And we can run errands for you. And we'll do anything else you need to have done," Marisol added.

Mrs. Blanco thought for a few seconds and then she said, "All right, girls. If you help me, then I'll have time to make Marisol's costume."

On the morning of Carnival Tuesday, Mrs. Blanco gave Marisol her costume. It was beautiful. "Thank you! Thank you!" Marisol told Mrs. Blanco and hugged her.

Go On ▶

The music blared loudly in the streets, The two girls walked toward the group Marisol was joining to be in a parade. Her costume shimmered in the bright Caribbean sunlight. "I feel like a princess," she told Nicolette.

"You look like a princess too, thanks to my grandmother," said Nicolette.

"She's *your* grandmother, and she's *my* fairy godmother," Marisol said with a smile.

© Macmillan/McGraw-Hill

Student Name _____

**Now answer Numbers 1 through 9 on your Answer Sheet.
Base your answers on the story "A Carnival Costume."**

1 Read this sentence from the story.

> **"Do you want an elegant, fancy costume?"**
> **Nicolette asked.**

The word *elegant* means

A. funny.

B. stylish.

C. expensive.

D. handmade.

2 Read this sentence from the story.

> **"Well, that would be irresistible."**

The suffix *-ible* tells you that *irresistible* is

F. an adverb.

G. an adjective.

H. a plural verb.

I. a plural noun.

3 Read this sentence from the story.

> **As they worked, they gossiped about the people
> in their neighborhood.**

What does *gossiped* mean?

A. argued

B. talked loudly

C. told stories about others

D. spoke seriously to each other

4 Read this sentence from the story.

> **Throwing feathers into the air, mischievous kids ran in and out of the racks of brightly colored skirts and tops.**

From the suffix *-ous,* you can tell that *mischievous* means

  F. full of mischief.

  G. without mischief.

  H. with less mischief.

  I. unable to do mischief.

5 Read this sentence from the story.

> **"Running like that is forbidden in Mrs. Blanco's store."**

What does the word *forbidden* mean?

  A. expected

  B. not usual

  C. dangerous

  D. not allowed

6 When the story begins, what is Marisol's problem?

  F. She has a costume for Carnival, but she wants a nicer one.

  G. She has a costume for Carnival, but her parents will not let her go.

  H. She wants a costume for Carnival, but she is too busy to make one.

  I. She wants a costume for Carnival, but she does not have the money to buy one.

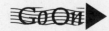

7 How does Marisol FIRST try to solve her problem?

   A. She and Nicolette make a costume.

   B. She asks her parents to buy her a better costume.

   C. She and Nicolette convince Marisol's parents to let her go to Carnival.

   D. She asks Nicolette to do her work so she will have more time at Carnival.

8 What does Marisol do NEXT?

   F. She decides not to go to Carnival.

   G. She pays Mrs. Blanco to make her a costume.

   H. She helps Mrs. Blanco in exchange for a costume.

   I. She and Nicolette borrow a costume from Mrs. Blanco.

Go On ▶

9 Explain why Marisol is a good problem solver. Use details from the story to support your answer.

READ
THINK
EXPLAIN

_____

_____

_____

_____

_____

_____

_____

_____

_____

Student Name _____

Read and answer questions 10–12 on your Answer Sheet.

10 Which word is spelled incorrectly?

    A. bawl

    B. clause

    C. turmiol

    D. cautious

11 Read this sentence.

    The <u>scrawny</u> moving man had to <u>hoist</u> the <u>stowt</u> and heavy coffeepot to the <u>counter</u>.

Which underlined word is spelled incorrectly?

    F. hoist

    G. stowt

    H. counter

    I. scrawny

12 Read this sentence.

    After Rita takes a cool <u>mowthful</u> of water from the <u>turquoise</u> <u>fountain</u>, she <u>sprawls</u> on the lawn.

Which underlined word is spelled incorrectly?

    A. sprawls

    B. fountain

    C. turquoise

    D. mowthful

Student Name _____

Read and answer questions 13–15 on your Answer Sheet.

13 In which sentence below is all **punctuation** correct?

    F. The ponys mane is very tangled.

    G. The two girls' coats are the same.

    H. The childs' feelings have been hurt.

14 Which sentence below is written correctly?

    A. The skys color is beautiful at night.

    B. I have fantasies of visiting the stars one day.

    C. I gaze at the sky and think about the stars mysteries.

Go On ▶

Student Name _____

15 Read the sentence in the box.

> **The dogs collar is too large.**

Which word should replace "dogs" in the sentence in the box?

F. dog's

G. dogs'

H. dogs's

© Macmillan/McGraw–Hill

Student Name _____

Student Evaluation Chart

Tested Skills	Number Correct	Percent Correct
Vocabulary Strategies: *Context clues,* 1, 3, 5; *suffixes,* 2, 4	/5	%
Reading Comprehension: *Problem and solution,* 6, 7, 8	/3	%
Short response: *Problem and solution,* 9	/2	%
Spelling: *Words with /ô/, /ou/, and /oi/,* 10, 11, 12	/3	%
Grammar, Mechanics, and Usage: *Possessive nouns,* 13, 15; *adding* s or 's, 14	/3	%
Total Weekly Test Score	**/16**	**%**

Correlations

Item	FCAT Assessed Benchmarks*	New Sunshine State Standards
1	LA.A.1.2.3	LA.5.1.6.3
2	LA.A.1.2.3	LA.5.1.6.7
3	LA.A.1.2.3	LA.5.1.6.3
4	LA.A.1.2.3	LA.5.1.6.7
5	LA.A.1.2.3	LA.5.1.6.3
6	LA.E.1.2.2	LA.5.2.1.2
7	LA.E.1.2.2	LA.5.2.1.2
8	LA.E.1.2.2	LA.5.2.1.2
9	LA.E.1.2.2	LA.5.2.1.2
10		LA.5.3.4.1
11		LA.5.3.4.1
12		LA.5.3.4.1
13		LA.5.3.4.4
14		LA.5.3.4.4
15		LA.5.3.4.4

* See benchmarks and standards on pages 379–384.

Name _____

Date _____

FLORIDA
Treasures

FCAT Format Weekly Assessment

TESTED SKILLS AND STRATEGIES

- **Vocabulary Strategies**
- **Reading Comprehension**
- **Spelling**
- **Grammar, Mechanics, and Usage**

Macmillan
McGraw-Hill

**Read the story "Raymond" before answering
Numbers 1 through 9.**

Raymond

The sun was just about to slip down below the horizon. Carlton stopped peeling potatoes for a moment. He took in the streaks of orange, pink, and lavender splashed across the sky. For a few seconds, it appeared to him that all movement stopped, both of humans and of animals. Even time appeared to be suspended.

Then Hank, the ranch boss, called his name, and everything returned to normal. "You better get those potatoes boiling," he said. "They'll be getting back any minute."

Hank was referring to the four cowboys who worked on the XIT Ranch. They had been out all day looking after the cattle. The ranch boss had set up camp 60 miles from the ranch house. Carlton was the ranch hand in charge of the cooking at the camp.

A short time later Carlton heard horses' hooves and familiar voices in the distance. In the last light of day, he saw Raymond and the other cowboys approaching. They looked almost tiny in the vastness of the plains. Of the four cowboys, Raymond was Carlton's favorite. He had worked on ranches for over 40 years, and Carlton loved listening to his stories.

Carlton sat with the men around a big campfire. They ate the simple meal he had fixed and talked about their work that day.

"It took me an hour to rescue a calf from a ravine—probably the deepest one around here," Tom said. The section of the XIT where they were was full of the narrow, rocky valleys. They made the cowboys' work hard and sometimes dangerous.

"I'll tell you the toughest part of *my* day," said Jimmy. "It was when something spooked those three cows and they swerved from the herd. By the time I caught up with them, they'd run a long way in the wrong direction."

"But Raymond got to them before you," Pete said, teasing Jimmy. Carlton pictured Raymond beating Jimmy to the three cows. Even though he was well over 60, Raymond rode with a graceful style. And the way he rode, or did anything else at the ranch, showed his enthusiasm. Maybe that was why Carlton admired him so much. Raymond had a passion for his work.

As the campfire flickered in the warm breeze, Carlton looked at the older man's face. Over the years, the sun and cold had etched deep creases in it. It looked peaceful, but Carlton wondered if Raymond thought about the future. There had been talk of replacing the horses with all-terrain vehicles. Carlton sensed that the continued presence of men like Raymond on the XIT was none too certain. Someone with many fewer skills could easily replace him.

Carlton looked down at the campfire and sighed. He had remembered something Raymond had said a few evenings ago: "Nothing in life is certain except change."

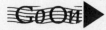

Student Name _____

**Now answer Numbers 1 through 9 on your Answer Sheet.
Base your answers on the story "Raymond."**

1 Read this sentence from the story.

> **Even time appeared to be suspended.**

What is the OPPOSITE of *suspended*?

A. hanging

B. stopped

C. speeding

D. confused

2 Read this sentence from the story.

> **They looked almost tiny in the vastness of
> the plains.**

Vastness is to _____ as *full* is to *empty*.

F. largeness

G. smallness

H. emptiness

I. timelessness

3 Read this sentence from the story.

> **"It took me an hour to rescue a calf from a ravine—
> probably the deepest one around here," Tom said.**

You can tell from the sentence that a *ravine* is a

A. wide field.

B. deep lake.

C. tall mountain.

D. narrow valley.

 GoOn

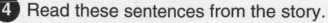
4 Read these sentences from the story.

> **Even though he was well over 60, Raymond rode with a graceful style. And the way he rode, or did anything else at the ranch, showed his enthusiasm.**

Enthusiasm is to _____ as *catch* is to *throw*.

F. boredom

G. confusion

H. eagerness

I. excitement

5 Read this sentence from the story.

> **Carlton sensed that the continued presence of men like Raymond on the XIT was none too certain.**

Which word below is the OPPOSITE of *presence*?

A. power

B. talents

C. absence

D. attendance

6 Which statement about Raymond PROBABLY is true?

F. He is worried about his future.

G. He likes talking about his work.

H. He sometimes feels bored with his work.

I. He believes that he is the best cowboy at the ranch.

© Macmillan/McGraw-Hill

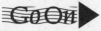

7 What can you infer about the characters in the story?

    A. The boss respects Raymond.

    B. Carlton is concerned for Raymond.

    C. The other cowboys are jealous of Raymond.

    D. Carlton would like Raymond to teach him to ride.

8 Which statement BEST describes ranch life today?

    F. Every ranch worker does similar work.

    G. Life on a ranch has changed little over time.

    H. As ranches change, different skills are needed.

    I. Most ranch hands eventually become cowboys.

Go On ▶

9 Working on a ranch involves many responsibilities. What type of person would make a good cowboy or cowgirl? Use details and information from the story to support your answer.

READ
THINK
EXPLAIN

_____

_____

_____

_____

_____

_____

_____

_____

Go On ▶

Student Name _____

Read and answer questions 10–12 on your Answer Sheet.

10 Which word is spelled incorrectly?

A. flater

B. mutter

C. jogger

D. empire

11 Read this sentence.

None of the horses could <u>gallop</u> through the <u>blizzard</u>, not even the <u>champoin</u> <u>mustang</u>.

Which underlined word is spelled incorrectly?

F. gallop

G. blizzard

H. mustang

I. champoin

12 Read this sentence.

The <u>vulture</u> circled above the <u>valley</u>, <u>fifteen</u> feet above the <u>kennell</u> where the dogs were sleeping.

Which underlined word is spelled incorrectly?

A. valley

B. fifteen

C. kennell

D. vulture

© Macmillan/McGraw-Hill

Student Name _____

The article below is a first draft that Thanh wrote for his teacher. Read the article to answer questions 13–15.

Dalmatians

→ ⬚1 Dalmations are very fast runners and can run for a long time.

→ ⬚2 A Dalmatian is the only breed of dog that seems to smile. ⬚3 A Dalmatian cannot actually smile like people do. ⬚4 But it can draw back its lips' because of unique muscles in its face. ⬚5 A Dalmatians owner likes to think that the dog is smiling at him or her.

→ ⬚6 To learn more interesting facts, read a book called The Wonderful Spotted Dog.

What do these mean?

| ⬚1 | This type of symbol is in the Florida test to show a sentence number. |

| → | This symbol in the test shows a new paragraph. |

The test may include the kinds of writing you might do. You will be asked to change and improve the writing.

Go On ▶

13 What is the correct way to write sentence [4]?

    F. But it can draw back its lips because of unique muscles in its face.

    G. But it can draw back its lips because of unique muscles' in its face.

    H. But it can draw back its lip's because of unique muscles' in its face.

    I. But it can draw back its lips' because of unique muscle's in its face.

14 Which word should replace "Dalmatians" in sentence [5]?

    A. Dalmatian

    B. Dalmatians'

    C. Dalmatian's

    D. Dalmatians's

15 What is the correct way to write sentence [6]?

    F. To learn more interesting facts, read a book called "The Wonderful Spotted Dog."

    G. To learn more interesting facts, read a book called *The wonderful spotted dog*.

    H. To learn more interesting facts, read a book called "the wonderful Spotted Dog."

    I. To learn more interesting facts, read a book called *The Wonderful Spotted Dog*.

STOP

Grade 5 • Unit 2 • Week 5
Student Evaluation Chart

Tested Skills	Number Correct	Percent Correct
Vocabulary Strategies: *Antonyms,*1, 5; *analogies: antonyms,* 2, 4; *context clues,* 3	/5	%
Reading Comprehension: *Plot development: make inferences,* 6, 7, 8	/3	%
Short response: *Plot development: make inferences,* 9	/2	%
Spelling: *VCCV pattern,* 10, 11, 12	/3	%
Grammar, Mechanics, and Usage: *Plural and possessives,* 13, 14; *punctuating titles,* 15	/3	%

Total Weekly Test Score	/16	%

Correlations

Item	FCAT Assessed Benchmarks*	New Sunshine State Standards
1	LA.A.1.2.3	LA.5.1.6.8
2	LA.A.1.2.3	LA.5.1.6.8
3	LA.A.1.2.3	LA.5.1.6.3
4	LA.A.1.2.3	LA.5.1.6.8
5	LA.A.1.2.3	LA.5.1.6.8
6	LA.E.1.2.2	LA.5.2.1.2
7	LA.E.1.2.2	LA.5.2.1.2
8	LA.A.2.2.1	LA.5.1.73
9	LA.A.2.2.1	LA.5.1.73
10		LA.5.3.4.1
11		LA.5.3.4.1
12		LA.5.3.4.1
13		LA.5.3.4.4
14		LA.5.3.4.4
15		LA.5.3.4.3

* See benchmarks and standards on pages 379–384.

FLORIDA

Treasures

FCAT Format Weekly Assessment

TESTED SKILLS AND STRATEGIES

- Vocabulary Strategies
- Reading Comprehension
- Spelling
- Grammar, Mechanics, and Usage

Mc Graw Hill **Macmillan McGraw-Hill**

Read the story "A Spy in the American Revolution" before answering Numbers 1 through 9.

A Spy in the American Revolution

"It's too dangerous, William. I can't allow you to do this," Mrs. Sommers said. She rubbed her hands together nervously.

"Ma, I'm 12 years old, and that is old enough. I want to support our soldiers in their fight against that tyrant King George. I want to help the Colonies become independent from Great Britain."

"William does have spunk," his older sister Mercy said. "Remember how he stood up to the Redcoats? Thanks to William's bravery, we were able to protect our animals."

Go On ▶

Mr. Sommers spoke up. "William is good at navigation and can find his way anywhere. And he learns quickly. People will be able to instruct him on how to help our cause."

The family continued discussing the matter through the night. By dawn Mr. and Mrs. Sommers had agreed to let their son spy for the American Colonies. They knew he would bring important information to the local leaders of the Revolution.

William rested for a while. Then he ate a warm meal, hugged his parents, and set off. He soon found the stark British camp. With a strong and confident swagger, he walked boldly into the camp. The soldiers took no notice of him.

William made a careful observation of the camp. He estimated that there were several hundred men. He saw cannons everywhere. He noticed that the British had a lot of flour and dried beef. "We could use those supplies," he thought.

He also listened to the men talking. He overheard one of the captains say that horses were being prepared. The troops were planning to set out that night. Some of the troops had already left. They were going to attack the patriots!

Go On ▶

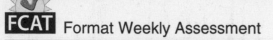

That evening William stole away from the British camp. A few hours later he was reporting to the Patriots what he had seen and heard among the British. "You're quite brave, boy," one of the colonial soldiers said. "Now we know when the enemy plans to attack and how well prepared they are."

William went on many other spy missions. At times the information he brought to the Patriots was extremely important. At other times it was less helpful. But at the end of every mission they praised him for his daring and his efforts. When he returned from his final mission, his father told him, "What a wonderful thing you've done for America, son." His father rarely gave compliments, and this remark made William beam.

A few years later, after the Patriots had won their cause, the governor of New Jersey gave William a medal for his work as a spy. Decades later, when William was an old man, he loved telling his grandchildren about the important part he had played in the American Revolution.

Student Name _____

Now answer Numbers 1 through 9 on your Answer Sheet. Base your answers on the story "A Spy in the American Revolution."

1 Read this sentence from the story.

> **"I want to support our soldiers in their fight against that tyrant King George."**

What is a *tyrant*?

A. a soldier

B. a Redcoat

C. a good king

D. an unfair ruler

2 Read these sentences from the story.

> **"William does have spunk," his older sister Mercy said. "Remember how he stood up to the Redcoats?"**

The word *spunk* means

F. fear.

G. money.

H. courage.

I. knowledge.

3 Read this sentence from the story.

> **"William is good at navigation and can find his way anywhere."**

Which word is NOT in the same word family as *navigation*?

A. naval

B. navigate

C. obligation

D. unnavigable

Go On

4 Read this sentence.

The British troops were going to attack the patriots.

Which word is NOT in the same word family as *patriots*?

F. patriotic

G. patriotism

H. patrolman

I. patriotically

5 Read this sentence from the story.

"People will be able to instruct him on how to help our cause."

Which word means almost the SAME as *instruct*?

A. teach

B. advise

C. correct

D. command

6 Which word BEST describes William?

F. shy

G. fearful

H. humble

I. determined

7 What is the MOST LIKELY reason that William is a successful spy?

    A. He is lucky and has a lot of help.

    B. He father has taught him how to be a spy.

    C. The British soldiers want to brag about their plans to him.

    D. The British soldiers do not notice him because he is young.

8 Which statement BEST describes the other members of William's family?

    F. They are loyal to the Colonial side in the war.

    G. They do not care about the Revolutionary War.

    H. They are secretly supporting the British in the war.

    I. They also are spies for the Colonial troops in the war.

Go On ▶

9 How can you tell that William is proud of his role in the American Revolution? Use details from the story to support your answer.

© Macmillan/McGraw-Hill

Go On

Student Name _____

Read and answers questions 10–12 on your Answer Sheet.

10 Which word is spelled incorrectly?

A. linen

B. loser

C. legel

D. humor

11 Read this sentence.

The <u>tyrant</u> was not a <u>desent</u> man, and he tried to <u>punish</u> the <u>local</u> people.

Which underlined word is spelled incorrectly?

F. local

G. tyrant

H. punish

I. desent

12 Read this sentence.

The <u>student</u> walked into the <u>cavarn</u>, which was <u>equal</u> in size to a <u>closet</u>.

Which underlined word is spelled incorrectly?

A. equal

B. closet

C. cavarn

D. student

Student Name _____

Read and answer questions 13–15 on your Answer Sheet.

13 Read the sentence in the box.

> Could it <u>be</u> that you are <u>afraid</u> to <u>fight</u>
> for the Patriots?

Which underlined word in the sentence in the box is an
action verb?

  F. be

  G. fight

  H. afraid

14 Which sentence below contains an **action verb**?

  A. Margaret felt dizzy.

  B. Keith smelled a skunk.

  C. Jaime was on first base.

15 Which sentence below is NOT written correctly?

    F. Artie wakes up early on Saturdays.

    G. Often he read a book or a magazine.

    H. If it is warm, he takes a walk in the park.

STOP

Student Name _____

Grade 5 • Unit 3 • Week 1
Student Evaluation Chart

Tested Skills	Number Correct	Percent Correct
Vocabulary Strategies: *Synonyms*, 1, 2, 5; *word families*, 3, 4	/5	%
Reading Comprehension: *Plot development: draw conclusions*, 6, 7, 8	/3	%
Short response: *Plot development: draw conclusions*, 9	/2	%
Spelling: *V/CV and VC/V patterns*, 10, 11, 12	/3	%
Grammar, Mechanics, and Usage: *Action verbs*, 13, 14; *subject-verb agreement*, 15	/3	%

Total Weekly Test Score	**/16**	**%**

Correlations

Item	FCAT Assessed Benchmarks*	New Sunshine State Standards
1	LA.A.1.2.3	LA.5.1.6.8
2	LA.A.1.2.3	LA.5.1.6.8
3	LA.A.1.2.3	LA.5.1.6.7
4	LA.A.1.2.3	LA.5.1.6.7
5	LA.A.1.2.3	LA.5.1.6.8
6	LA.E.1.2.2	LA.5.2.1.2
7	LA.E.1.2.2	LA.5.2.1.2
8	LA.E.1.2.2	LA.5.2.1.2
9	LA.E.1.2.2	LA.5.2.1.2
10		LA.5.3.4.1
11		LA.5.3.4.1
12		LA.5.3.4.1
13		LA.5.3.4.4
14		LA.5.3.4.4
15		LA.5.3.4.5

* See benchmarks and standards on pages 379–384.

Name _____

Date _____

FCAT Format Weekly Assessment

TESTED SKILLS AND STRATEGIES

- Vocabulary Strategies
- Reading Comprehension
- Spelling
- Grammar, Mechanics, and Usage

Macmillan
McGraw-Hill

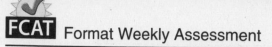
Read the article "The Nineteenth Amendment" before answering Numbers 1 through 9.

The Nineteenth Amendment

Women in the United States were not always allowed to vote. Instead, women had to fight for the right to vote. They wanted to be able to choose their own representatives and elect the people who shared their ideas. The struggle was difficult and long. It required many people working together to get women the right to vote. These people should be honored for their efforts.

In July 1848, a group of women met in Seneca Falls, New York, for the Women's Rights Convention. Susan B. Anthony, Lucy Stone, Lucretia Mott, Elizabeth Cady Stanton, and others joined together to fight for the right to vote. The women had to convince people that they should be allowed to take part in elections. Some people did not think that a woman could qualify to vote.

On March 3, 1913, about 8,000 people participated in a protest in Washington, D.C. The march was organized to call greater attention to the cause of women's voting rights.

© Macmillan/McGraw–Hill

Go On▶

For the next several decades, the women continued their struggle to be able to vote. They made gains in other areas besides voting. In 1870, a woman in Iowa became the first female attorney in the United States. In 1872, the U.S. Congress passed a law giving women who worked for the government equal pay for equal work. But in the area of voting rights, for a long time there were few gains. Women made speeches and held protest marches all over the country. Bullies tried to break up meetings and events, sometimes with success. However, the women did not submit. They did not even postpone or put off their work. Instead, they kept working courageously for their cause.

Finally, the speeches, marches, and meetings began to pay off. In some parts of the country, women were given the right to vote. In 1869, the Wyoming Territory became the first place in the United States to allow women to cast ballots. This was a satisfactory step, but it was only a start. Wyoming was only one territory. But other territories and states soon followed. In 1893, the Colorado legislature gave women the right to vote. Utah and Idaho did so in 1896. Women in the state of Washington were first allowed to take part in elections in 1910.

The battle was won in 1919, a very long time after it had started. That year the U.S. Congress passed the Nineteenth Amendment to the Constitution. It stated, "The right of citizens of the United States to vote shall not be denied or abridged by the United States or by any State on account of sex." A majority of the states had to ratify, or approve, the amendment. This was accomplished in 1920, and the Nineteenth Amendment became law.

Go On ▶

The work of courageous women such as Susan B. Anthony and so many others should be honored. Without such work, American women might have continued to be denied an important right for an even longer time.

Women proudly exercised their right to vote after the passage of the Nineteenth Amendment.

Go On ▶

Now answer Numbers 1 through 9 on your Answer Sheet. Base your answers on the article "The Nineteenth Amendment."

1 Read this dictionary entry.

> **at-tor-ney** (ə tûr´ nē) *Noun.* a lawyer

Which part of the dictionary entry tells you how to pronounce the word *attorney*?

A. noun

B. a lawyer

C. (ə tûr´ nē)

D. at-tor-ney

2 Read these sentences from the article.

> **Bullies tried to break up meetings and events, sometimes with success. However, the women did not submit.**

What does *submit* mean?

F. protest

G. give in

H. speak up

I. fight back

3 Read this sentence from the article.

> **They did not even postpone or put off their work.**

What does the word *postpone* mean in the sentence?

A. delay

B. ignore

C. cancel

D. prolong

4 Read this sentence from the article.

> **This was a satisfactory step, but it was only a start.**

Which word means almost the SAME as *satisfactory*?

F. good

G. difficult

H. passing

I. pleasant

5 Read this dictionary entry.

> **colo-nel** (kûr´ nəl) *Noun.* an army officer ranking below brigadier general

From the pronunciation key, you can tell that *colonel* has

A. 1 syllable.

B. 2 syllables.

C. 3 syllables.

D. 4 syllables.

6 Where does the author provide specific information about a protest march?

F. in the caption under the first drawing

G. in the caption under the second drawing

H. in the title "The Nineteenth Amendment"

I. in the first and last paragraphs of the article

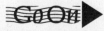

7 Which statement below BEST summarizes the article?

    A. The struggle for women to win the right to vote was difficult.

    B. Ceremonies were held to honor women like Susan B. Anthony.

    C. Before 1920, women who worked for the federal government could vote.

    D. The citizens of some states were reluctant to give women the right to vote.

8 Which statement from the article is an opinion?

    F. "These people should be honored for their efforts."

    G. "Women in the United States were not always allowed to vote."

    H. "In 1870, a woman in Iowa became the first female attorney in the United States."

    I. "Women in the state of Washington were first allowed to take part in elections in 1910."

9 "Women struggled for many years to win the right to vote."
Is this statement a fact or an opinion? Use information from
the article to explain your answer.

READ
THINK
EXPLAIN

_____

_____

_____

_____

_____

_____

_____

_____

_____

_____

_____

_____

_____

_____

_____

_____

_____

Go On

Student Name _____

Read and answer questions 10–12 on your Answer Sheet.

10 Which word is spelled incorrectly?

  A. feul

  B. cruel

  C. patriot

  D. meteor

11 Read this sentence.

  The <u>poet</u> read from her <u>diery</u>, showed a <u>video</u>, and played a song on the <u>piano</u>.

  Which underlined word is spelled incorrectly?

  F. poet

  G. diery

  H. video

  I. piano

12 Read this sentence.

  Bob listens to the <u>rodeo</u> on the <u>radeo</u> because he doesn't have time to <u>meander</u> over the entire <u>diameter</u> of the field.

  Which underlined word is spelled incorrectly?

  A. rodeo

  B. radeo

  C. diameter

  D. meander

Student Name _____

Read the newspaper article "New Zoo Opens." Choose the word or words that correctly complete questions 13 and 14.

New Zoo Opens

The citizens of Bellingham and visitors to our city have something new and exciting to do. They can go to the Lila Benavides Zoo, named for the woman whose generous donation made the zoo possible.

The opening was held last Saturday with speeches and special entertainment. More than 2,000 people (13) through the gates that day.

The zoo will be open Tuesday through Sunday from 1 p.m. to 7 p.m. Be sure to take a camera when you (14) to see this wonderful collection of animals.

13 Which answer should go in blank (13)?

F. pass

G. passed

H. will pass

14 Which answer should go in blank (14)?

A. go

B. went

C. have gone

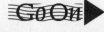

Student Name _____

Read and answer question 15 on your Answer Sheet.

15 Read the poem in the box.

> **See the Kitten on the wall,**
> **Sporting with the leaves that fall,**
> **Withered leaves—one—two—and three,**
> **From the lofty Elder-tree!**
>
> –*from* The Kitten and the Falling Leaves,
> *William Wordsworth (1770–1850)*

Why does the author end each of the first three lines of the poem in the box with a comma?

  F. to indicate that the reader should pause

  G. to indicate that each line is a complete thought

  H. to indicate that the reader should come to a stop

STOP

Student Name _____

Grade 5 • Unit 3 • Week 2
Student Evaluation Chart

Tested Skills	Number Correct	Percent Correct
Vocabulary Strategies: *Pronunciation key, 1, 5; context clues, 2, 3; synonyms, 4*	/5	%
Reading Comprehension: *Relevant facts and details, 6, 7, 8*	/3	%
Extended response: *Relevant facts and details, 9*	/4	%
Spelling: *V/V pattern, 10, 11, 12*	/3	%
Grammar, Mechanics, and Usage: *Verb tenses, 13, 14; capitalization and punctuation in poetry, 15*	/3	%

Total Weekly Test Score	/18	%

Correlations

Item	FCAT Assessed Benchmarks*	New Sunshine State Standards
1		LA.5.1.6.10
2	LA.A.1.2.3	LA.5.1.6.3
3	LA.A.1.2.3	LA.5.1.6.3
4	LA.A.1.2.3	LA.5.1.6.8
5		LA.5.1.6.10
6	LA.A.2.2.1	LA.5.2.2.2
7	LA.A.2.2.1	LA.5.2.2.2
8	LA.A.2.2.1	LA.5.2.2.2
9	LA.A.2.2.1	LA.5.2.2.2
10		LA.5.3.4.1
11		LA.5.3.4.1
12		LA.5.3.4.1
13		LA.5.3.4.4
14		LA.5.3.4.4
15		LA.5.3.4.3

* See benchmarks and standards on pages 379–384.

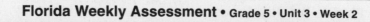

Name _____

Date _____

 Format
Weekly
Assessment

TESTED SKILLS AND STRATEGIES

- Vocabulary Strategies
- Reading Comprehension
- Spelling
- Grammar, Mechanics, and Usage

Read the article "What You Can Do" before answering Numbers 1 through 9.

What You Can Do

Human actions change the world. Every person in the world uses and depends on its natural resources. However, by using as few of these materials as possible, humanity can reduce harmful effects to nature. Everyone should be willing to do his or her part. Damage to the world should not go unheeded.

Water is needed for life, and many people use a lot of water. There are simple things you can do to use less water. A special showerhead can cut the amount of shower water you use in half. The average person in the United States uses about 15 gallons of water for one shower, so using the special showerhead can save 2,747 gallons of water per year. There are several other ways you can conserve water at home,

too. You can take shorter showers and turn off the tap while brushing your teeth. You also can inspect your home for leaks; if you find one, repair it promptly.

Electricity runs the machines in our homes and makes it possible to turn on lights, and Americans use a lot of electricity. Energy is needed to create electricity, and the prevailing sources of that energy are fuels such as oil and coal, which are relatively abundant. Burning fuels makes the air dirty. Dirty air can cause people to have lung problems. However, it is possible to reduce the amount of fuels that are being burned. What can you do? Buy energy-saving models of machines like ovens and refrigerators. Turn off lights when they are not needed. Finally, keep your home a little warmer in the summer and a little cooler in the winter. When you do this, you can adapt to the indoor temperature by wearing appropriate clothes. By turning down the heat and air conditioning you can improve the world—and save money, too!

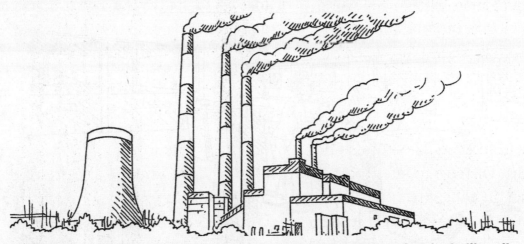

Using less electricity reduces the pollution caused by burning fuels like oil and coal.

Saving water and electricity are not the only things you can do to protect the environment. Reusing materials is also helpful. It is inevitable that people will need and use items made of paper, plastic, and rubber. After these items are used, they can be brought to a recycling center. The center will take paper or plastic goods and turn them into something new. White paper is made into notebook paper, and notebook paper is changed into newspaper. Plastic soda bottles may be made into plastic boards that are used to manufacture benches and build decks. Old car tires are chopped into tiny pieces and mixed into materials used to make and strengthen roads.

Changing the ways you use electricity, water, and materials may seem difficult at first. But once you are enlightened about the benefits of saving and recycling, you will realize how important it is to be aware of your actions.

In many cities, recycling centers are located in convenient places. The people in charge of the centers usually make them easy to use.

**Now answer Numbers 1 through 9 on your Answer Sheet.
Base your answers on the article "What You Can Do."**

1 Read this sentence from the article.

Damage to the world should not go unheeded.

The prefix *un-* tells you that *unheeded* means

A. noticed.

B. not noticed.

C. noticed again.

D. noticed before.

2 Read this sentence from the article.

**Energy is needed to create electricity, and the
prevailing sources of that energy are fuels such
as oil and coal, which are relatively abundant.**

Which word means almost the SAME as *prevailing*?

F. scarce   **H.** common

G. unusual   **I.** expensive

3 Read this sentence from the article.

**It is inevitable that people will need and use things
made of paper, plastic, and rubber.**

Which word means almost the SAME as *inevitable*?

A. unlikely

B. avoidable

C. uncertain

D. expected

4 Read this sentence from the article.

But once you are enlightened about the benefits of saving and recycling, you will realize how important it is to be aware of your actions.

The word *enlightened* means almost the SAME as

F. engaged.

G. lightened.

H. instructed.

I. brightened.

5 Which word from the article has a prefix that means "again"?

A. realize

B. reduce

C. reusing

D. resources

6 Which statement from the article is the author's opinion?

F. "Everyone should be willing to do his or her part."

G. "Dirty air can cause people to have lung problems."

H. "Water is needed for life, and many people use a lot of water."

I. "Every person in the world uses and depends on its natural resources."

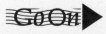

7 The author mentions taking shorter showers to support the claim that

    A. many people leave the tap on while brushing their teeth.

    B. there are simple things people can do to reduce water use.

    C. the average American uses about 15 gallons of water during a shower.

    D. special showerheads can reduce by half the amount of shower water used.

8 Which word is MOST LIKELY to help persuade readers to recycle?

    F. cities

    G. located

    H. usually

    I. convenient

Go On ▶

9 What is the author of "What You Can Do" trying to persuade readers to do? How does the author do this? Use details and information from the article to support your answer.

READ
THINK
EXPLAIN

_____

_____

_____

_____

_____

_____

_____

_____

_____

Go On ▶

Student Name _____

Read and answer questions 10–12 on your Answer Sheet.

10 Which word is spelled incorrectly?

   A. address

   B. improve

   C. concrete

   D. allthough

11 Read this sentence.

The <u>handsome</u> <u>fiddler</u> did not <u>complane</u> about playing a second show at the <u>fairground</u>.

Which underlined word is spelled incorrectly?

   F. fiddler

   G. complane

   H. handsome

   I. fairground

12 Read this sentence.

The camper saw a <u>footprint</u> on the <u>grasland</u> on the <u>hilltop</u> and figured it belonged to her hiking <u>partner</u>.

Which underlined word is spelled incorrectly?

   A. hilltop

   B. partner

   C. footprint

   D. grasland

Student Name _____

Read the school newspaper article "Use Your School Library." Choose the word or words that correctly complete questions 13 and 14.

Use Your School Library

Ms. Linder, our school librarian, has an important message for students: "Use your library more often. The library is here to help you do well in school." She says that fewer students (13) into the library this year than any other year.

Ms. Linder wants students to know something else. The library (14) only for helping you make good grades. "It's also here to make your life more enjoyable," says the librarian. "There are so many interesting, wonderful books to choose from."

13 Which answer should go in blank (13)?

F. come

G. have came

H. have come

14 Which answer should go in blank (14)?

A. isn't

B. isnt'

C. isn't

Read and answer question 15 on your Answer Sheet.

15 Which sentence below is NOT written correctly?

    F. Teresa been practicing all week for the soccer match.

    G. Her parents have encouraged her to do her very best.

    H. Her coach will give her advice right before the soccer match starts.

STOP

Grade 5 • Unit 3 • Week 3
Student Evaluation Chart

Tested Skills	Number Correct	Percent Correct
Vocabulary Strategies: *Prefixes,*1, 5; *synonyms,* 2, 3, 4	/5	%
Reading Comprehension: *Author's purpose: persuade,* 6, 7, 8	/3	%
Short response: *Author's purpose: persuade,* 9	/2	%
Spelling: *VCCCV pattern,* 10, 11, 12	/3	%
Grammar, Mechanics, and Usage: *Main and helping verbs,* 13, 15; *contractions,* 14	/3	%

Total Weekly Test Score	/16	%

Correlations		
Item	FCAT Assessed Benchmarks*	New Sunshine State Standards
1	LA.A.1.2.3	LA.5.1.6.7
2	LA.A.1.2.3	LA.5.1.6.8
3	LA.A.1.2.3	LA.5.1.6.8
4	LA.A.1.2.3	LA.5.1.6.8
5	LA.A.1.2.3	LA.5.1.6.7
6	LA.A.2.2.2	LA.5.1.7.2
7	LA.A.2.2.2	LA.5.1.7.2
8	LA.A.2.2.2	LA.5.1.7.2
9	LA.A.2.2.2	LA.5.1.7.2
10		LA.5.3.4.1
11		LA.5.3.4.1
12		LA.5.3.4.1
13		LA.5.3.4.4
14		LA.5.3.4.3
15		LA.5.3.4.4

* See benchmarks and standards on pages 379–384.

© Macmillan/McGraw–Hill

Name _____

Date _____

 **Format
Weekly
Assessment**

TESTED SKILLS AND STRATEGIES

- **Vocabulary Strategies**
- **Reading Comprehension**
- **Spelling**
- **Grammar, Mechanics, and Usage**

Read the story "Life with Trees" before answering Numbers 1 through 9.

Life with Trees

Matthew Macafee was a kind of criminal. He didn't rob banks or hurt people directly. Instead, his crimes were against nature.

Matthew owned many factories. His factories gushed chemicals into nearby rivers, and he did nothing to stop it. He lived on a large estate, but he didn't take care of the forests that were on his land. Over the years, he had cut down trees to sell them for lumber without replacing them. Only one forest area of some scrawny and gnarled trees remained on the now parched land, land that had once been lush and brimming with life.

Matthew's servant, Ito, remembered what the estate had been like long ago. That was when Matthew's father had owned the land. Matthew's father had planted most of the trees that Matthew now ordered to be cut down.

Matthew was cold-hearted. He also was rich and quite content with his life—until one particular day, that is.

On that hot summer day, he was in the last remaining forest area on his estate, marking trees to be cut down. He grew tired in the scorching heat, and he dozed off in the shade of a dying oak tree. He dreamed that the few trees around him were talking to him.

© Macmillan/McGraw–Hill

"Harsh winds will destroy your house," a sickly pine tree said.

"You are going to pay for your crimes," the dying oak tree warned him.

Matthew felt a rustling behind him. The oak tree loomed menacingly over him. "Remember this lesson," the tree continued. "You cannot destroy nature without paying a price."

"I didn't do anything wrong!" Matthew shouted.

"That is far from the truth," the oak tree said sadly.

Matthew awoke feeling awful. He thought, "I *have* been acting irresponsibly. It's time to change." And at that very moment he decided to live his life differently.

Before the year was over, he had closed down his factories. He also had changed much of his estate to parkland. He bought hundreds of trees and had them planted. In time, they grew and attracted birds and other wildlife.

Go On ▶

One day Matthew was taking his usual stroll through the beautiful landscape of his estate. With him was his servant Ito, who was now quite old. Matthew asked Ito, "Why should I be the only one to enjoy these flowers and hear these birds sing? I'm going to turn most of my estate into a public park."

Ito had a sudden, strong memory of Matthew's father and smiled. When Matthew had become very old, he went to bed late one night. The next morning Ito's son Akira came to wake him up. But, to the young man's astonishment, Matthew was gone. In his place was a small oak tree. Akira planted the tree in the public park, where it grew tall and strong. People who visit the park say they can hear the oak singing happily in the wind.

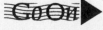

Now answer Numbers 1 through 9 on your Answer Sheet. Base your answers on the story "Life with Trees."

1 Read this sentence from the story.

> **His factories gushed chemicals into nearby rivers, and he did nothing to stop it.**

In the sentence, the word *gushed* emphasizes

A. the type of the chemicals.

B. the amount of the chemicals.

C. the strength of the chemicals.

D. the harshness of the chemicals.

2 Read this sentence.

> **The scrawny dog looked as though it had not eaten for days.**

Which word below is the connotation for *scrawny* as it is used in the sentence?

F. slim   **H.** hungry

G. bony   **I.** slender

3 Read this sentence.

> **Only one forest area of gnarled trees remained on the estate.**

Which word means about the SAME as *gnarled*?

A. ugly   **C.** straight

B. broken   **D.** crooked

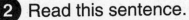

4 Read this sentence.

Mostly cactus grew on the parched land.

Which word means about the SAME as *parched*?

F. dry

G. distant

H. colorful

I. dangerous

5 Read this sentence.

Matthew gave his servant a scorching glare and told him to hurry.

What is the connotation of *scorching* in the sentence?

A. dry

B. hot

C. angry

D. rough

6 In the beginning of the story, Matthew is compared to

F. a criminal.

G. a land owner.

H. a rich person.

I. a happy person.

7 What is the MOST important difference between Matthew and his father?

    A. the way they have treated the land

    B. the way they have treated their servant

    C. how much money they have made from the land

    D. how old they are when they are in charge of the land

8 Which statement BEST shows how Matthew changes in the story?

    F. He plants hundreds of trees.

    G. He regularly takes walks on his estate.

    H. He has a disturbing dream in which trees talk to him.

    I. He decides to turn part of his estate into a public park.

9 Matthew goes through a change during this story. Use details from the story to explain:

READ
THINK
EXPLAIN

- what Matthew is like at the beginning of the story, and
- how he has changed by the end of the story

_____
_____
_____
_____
_____
_____
_____
_____
_____
_____
_____
_____
_____
_____
_____
_____
_____

Go On ▶

Student Name _____

Read and answer questions 10–12 on your Answer Sheet.

10 Which word is spelled incorrectly?

    A. flurry

    B. coastal

    C. seeson

    D. reserve

11 Read this sentence.

> A <u>dozen</u> children watched the <u>expurt</u> <u>restore</u> the <u>cocoon</u> to its tree.

Which underlined word is spelled incorrectly?

    F. dozen

    G. expurt

    H. restore

    I. cocoon

12 Read this sentence.

> If a <u>pithon</u> is <u>beside</u> you and wants to <u>embrace</u> you, get <u>active</u> and run away!

Which underlined word is spelled incorrectly?

    A. active

    B. pithon

    C. beside

    D. embrace

Go On ▶

Read and answer questions 13–15 on your Answer Sheet.

13 Read the sentence in the box.

┌───┐
│ The <u>desert</u> <u>seems</u> <u>empty</u> of life. │
└───┘

Which underlined word in the sentence in the box is a
linking verb?

F. empty

G. desert

H. seems

14 Which sentence below contains a **linking verb**?

A. Jorge tasted the delicious spaghetti.

B. Suzie connected the dots on the picture.

C. Su-Jung did not appear well after the long hike.

Go On ▶

15 Which sentence below contains an error in **punctuation**?

   F. Kathy looked at her brother Trevor and asked, "Did you hear something?"

   G. "It sounded like breaking glass", Trevor answered.

   H. Kathy paused, then said, "Maybe we should go check it out."

STOP

Grade 5 · Unit 3 · Week 4
Student Evaluation Chart

Tested Skills	Number Correct	Percent Correct
Vocabulary Strategies: *Denotation/ connotation, 1, 2, 5; synonyms 3, 4*	/5	%
Reading Comprehension: *Compare characters, 6, 7, 8*	/3	%
Extended response: *Compare characters, 9*	/4	%
Spelling: *Accented syllables, 10, 11, 12*	/3	%
Grammar, Mechanics, and Usage: *Linking verbs, 13, 14; use quotation marks in dialogue, 15*	/3	%
Total Weekly Test Score	/18	%

Correlations

Item	FCAT Assessed Benchmarks*	New Sunshine State Standards
1	LA.A.1.2.3	LA.5.1.6.9
2	LA.A.1.2.3	LA.5.1.6.9
3	LA.A.1.2.3	LA.5.1.6.8
4	LA.A.1.2.3	LA.5.1.6.8
5	LA.A.1.2.3	LA.5.1.6.9
6	LA.E.1.2.2	LA.5.2.1.2
7	LA.E.1.2.2	LA.5.2.1.2
8	LA.E.1.2.2	LA.5.2.1.2
9	LA.E.1.2.2	LA.5.2.1.2
10		LA.5.3.4.1
11		LA.5.3.4.1
12		LA.5.3.4.1
13		LA.5.3.4.4
14		LA.5.3.4.4
15		LA.5.3.4.3

* See benchmarks and standards on pages 379–384.

Name _____

Date _____

FCAT Format Weekly Assessment

TESTED SKILLS AND STRATEGIES

- **Vocabulary Strategies**
- **Reading Comprehension**
- **Spelling**
- **Grammar, Mechanics, and Usage**

Macmillan
McGraw-Hill

Read the story "A Saturday Morning Adventure" before answering Numbers 1 through 9.

A Saturday Morning Adventure

"These new video games are really cool," Rasheed says. He and his friend Jami play video games almost every weekend. They fly in their own spaceships to the game port 500 miles away. It takes them ten minutes to get there.

Rasheed and Jami like the games that take place in outer space the best. On this particular Saturday, the two kids are playing "Space Attack." In this game, meteors zoom from outer space into Earth's atmosphere, and attack ships try to hit the players' ship.

"Look," Jami says. "I just reversed course. Maybe if I go the opposite way my spaceship won't get smashed. It's a good thing we have our space suits on. If our ship gets hit by a meteor, we can just float through space until a robot rescues us."

"To continue paying for an additional minute, please pay 100 more tokens at this time," says the robot running the game room.

Go On ▶

"Will do," says Rasheed, and he hands the robot the tokens. The machine looks just like a real person. "These new robots can do anything. They're so much better than the old-fashioned robots of the last century."

"You can say *that* again," says Jami. "My grandfather told me stories about the robots that people used when he was young. They had jerky movements, and they talked in a funny way. My grandfather makes me laugh when he imitates them."

Suddenly Rasheed screams, "Look out! That attack ship just rotated and turned around. Now it's headed right toward us!"

Jami calmly pulls up on her joystick. "This is easy," she says with a laugh. But her laugh is cut off by the gasp she makes when the joystick fails to respond. "This joystick is defective!" she yells. "The attack ship is gaining on us!"

Rasheed adjusts the dials to increase their speed, but the ship still can't move fast enough to avoid the attack. With a sickening thud, the attack ship hits theirs. Jami is thrown forward and then staggers back into her seat. Rasheed is dangling from the ceiling and holding onto his seat belt.

But Jami doesn't panic. She checks to make sure that her space suit hasn't been damaged. Next she asks Rasheed if he's hurt and tells him to check his space suit. Then she calmly she takes out her tools. She repairs the joystick and adjusts the dials. "All fixed," she announces. She calmly steers the ship into dock.

When the kids are getting into their own spaceship, Rasheed makes a suggestion. "Maybe next week we can go laser-bowling instead of playing video games."

"No way!" Jami says. "Compared to these new video games, laser-bowling is way too boring!"

© Macmillan/McGraw-Hill

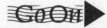

Now answer Numbers 1 through 9 on your Answer Sheet. Base your answers on the story "A Saturday Morning Adventure."

1 Read these sentences from the story.

> **"I just reversed course. Maybe if I go the opposite way my spaceship won't get smashed."**

Which word or phrase means about the SAME as *reversed*?

A. completed

B. went faster

C. made no change

D. changed direction

2 Read this sentence from the story.

> **"That attack ship just rotated and turned around."**

Rotated is to *revolved* as *staggered* is to

F. staged.   **H.** walked.

G. played.   **I.** swayed.

3 Read this sentence from the story.

> **"This joystick is defective!"**

Which word means about the SAME as *defective*?

A. old   **C.** turned off

B. broken   **D.** incomplete

Go On ▶

4 Read this sentence from the story.

> **Rasheed is dangling from the ceiling and holding onto his seat belt.**

Bug is to *insect* as *dangling* is to

  F. tearing.

  G. fighting.

  H. hanging.

  I. breaking.

5 What can you conclude about the game "Space Attack"?

  A. It is realistic.

  B. It is not realistic.

  C. It is inexpensive.

  D. It has real battles.

6 When do the events of this story take place?

  F. in the past

  G. in a dream

  H. in the future

  I. in the present

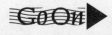

7 What is the BEST way to describe Jami?

   A. She stays calm under pressure.

   B. She sometimes jumps to conclusions.

   C. She often panics in difficult situations.

   D. She needs more practice repairing things.

8 Based on the story, what can you conclude about Jami and Rasheed?

   F. Jami likes adventure more than Rasheed does.

   G. Rasheed likes to be in charge more than Jami does.

   H. Jami and Rasheed have been friends for many years.

   I. Rasheed and Jami often disagree on how to solve a problem.

Go On ▶

9 What conclusion can you draw about the type of person Rasheed is? Use details and information from the story in your answer.

READ
THINK
EXPLAIN

_____

_____

_____

_____

_____

_____

_____

_____

_____

Go On ▶

Student Name _____

Read and answer questions 10–12 on your Answer Sheet.

10 Which word is spelled incorrectly?

    A. pillar
    B. shatter
    C. directur
    D. scissors

11 Read this sentence.

> The <u>professor</u> is a <u>scholar</u> who travels to the <u>equator</u> to study a <u>cratar</u> in a volcano.

Which underlined word is spelled incorrectly?

    F. cratar
    G. scholar
    H. equator
    I. professor

12 Read this sentence.

> The <u>commander</u> spoke with the <u>soldier</u> about asking the <u>governer</u> for help correcting the <u>error</u>.

Which underlined word is spelled incorrectly?

    A. error
    B. soldier
    C. governer
    D. commander

The story below is a first draft that Maritza wrote for her teacher. Read the article to answer questions 13–15.

A Hurt Student

→ [1] Keiko ran into the nurse's office and speaked loudly. [2] "Christie fell off the slide and hurt herself badly!"

→ [3] Ms. Shapiro, the school nurse, stayed calm. [4] She heared such things many times before. [5] She got some supplies and said, "Take me to Christie."

→ [6] They went to the playground. [7] The nurse bended down and begun to ask Christie questions. [8] Then she gently moved her arm. "It's a sprain, but it's not broken."

What do these mean?

[1] This type of symbol is in the Florida test to show a sentence number.

→ This symbol in the test shows a new paragraph.

The test may include the kinds of writing you might do. You will be asked to change and improve the writing.

Go On ▶

Student Name _____

13 What is the correct way to write sentence ☐1?

    F. Keiko run into the nurse's office and spoke loudly.

    G. Keiko ran into the nurse's office and spoke loudly.

    H. Keiko runned into the nurse's office and spoke loudly.

    I. Keiko runned into the nurse's office and speaked loudly.

14 What is the correct way to write sentence ☐4?

    A. She hears such things many times before.

    B. She had heard such things many times before.

    C. She has hearing such things many times before.

    D. She was hearing such things many times before.

15 What is the correct way to write sentence ☐7?

    F. The nurse bent down and began to ask
       Christie questions.

    G. The nurse bent down and begun to ask
       Christie questions.

    H. The nurse bended down and begin to ask
       Christie questions.

    I. The nurse bended down and began to ask
       Christie questions.

STOP

Student Name _____

Student Evaluation Chart

Tested Skills	Number Correct	Percent Correct
Vocabulary Strategies: *Context clues*, 1; *analogies*, 2, 4; *synonyms*, 3	/4	%
Reading Comprehension: *Plot development: draw conclusions*, 5, 6, 7, 8	/4	%
Short response: *Plot development: draw conclusions*, 9	/2	%
Spelling: *Accented syllables*, 10, 11, 12	/3	%
Grammar, Mechanics, and Usage: *Irregular verbs*, 13, 15; *correct verb usage*, 14	/3	%
Total Weekly Test Score	/16	%

Correlations

Item	FCAT Assessed Benchmarks*	New Sunshine State Standards
1	LA.A.1.2.3	LA.5.1.6.3
2	LA.A.1.2.3	LA.5.1.6.8
3	LA.A.1.2.3	LA.5.1.6.8
4	LA.A.1.2.3	LA.5.1.6.8
5	LA.E.1.2.2	LA.5.2.1.2
6	LA.E.1.2.2	LA.5.2.1.2
7	LA.E.1.2.2	LA.5.2.1.2
8	LA.E.1.2.2	LA.5.2.1.2
9	LA.E.1.2.2	LA.5.2.1.2
10		LA.5.3.4.1
11		LA.5.3.4.1
12		LA.5.3.4.1
13		LA.5.3.4.4
14		LA.5.3.4.4
15		LA.5.3.4.4

* See benchmarks and standards
on pages 379–384.

Name _____

Date _____

FCAT Format Weekly Assessment

TESTED SKILLS AND STRATEGIES

- **Vocabulary Strategies**
- **Reading Comprehension**
- **Spelling**
- **Grammar, Mechanics, and Usage**

Macmillan
McGraw-Hill

Read the story "Six Brave Students" before answering Numbers 1 through 9.

Six Brave Students

September 15, 1958, was not an ordinary day for Cathy Washington and five other children in Tennessee. On this day they would become the first African-American students to attend the Bluebell Lane School.

It was a spectacular day, with the sun shining brightly in a clear blue sky. "At least the weather is on our side," said Cathy to her companions. They laughed feebly. But they recognized the dangerous battle they were facing to obtain their right to an education.

The children got on the public bus and paid their fares. On the route to school, they saw many angry people lined up in the street. The protesters raised tightly clenched fists. "Go home!" they yelled. "We don't want you here. Go back to your own school on your side of town."

"We belong here," Cathy blurted out, even though the people on the street couldn't hear her. Then she calmed down a bit and said, "Four years ago, the Supreme Court said that we can get an education with white students. We don't need your permission to attend your school because it's our school as well." She spoke as if she were practicing something that she planned to say to a crowd of people.

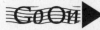

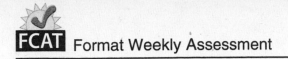

Cathy's friend Tyrone eyed the other passengers and said nervously, "Cathy, stop talking. We don't want to do anything that might cause even more trouble. I feel enough trouble in the air already."

At the school, a mob of people yelled. A few threw rotten pieces of fruit. Police officers tried to keep the peace. Although Cathy and the other children were fearful, they did not show it, and they certainly did not change their minds about the historic action they were about to take. As they walked bravely to the school entrance, Cathy glanced at the words over the door. She read aloud the school motto that was chiseled in stone. "With equality for all," it said.

 Go On

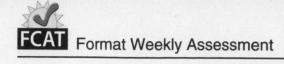

The six African-American students held their heads high as they walked into the building. All of them knew that this was only the beginning of the battle. They also realized that while some white students would become their friends, others never would.

Those six students persevered and completed their education at the Bluebell Lane School. Many years later, one of their former classmates asked Cathy for her autograph.

"Why do you want my signature?" Cathy asked the white woman.

"Because I admire your courage," the woman replied. "You were only a child, but you stood up for your rights on that sunny day in September. I've been a teacher for 15 years, Cathy. And by now I've told hundreds of students about what you did at that school. For them, you're a hero."

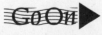

Student Name _____

Now answer Numbers 1 through 9 on your Answer Sheet.
Base your answers on the story "Six Brave Students."

1 Read this sentence.

The fare for the bus is two dollars.

What does the word *fare* mean?

A. cost

B. clear

C. exhibition

D. passenger

2 Read this sentence from the story.

The protesters raised tightly clenched fists.

What does *clenched* mean?

F. closed

G. opened

H. relaxed

I. changed

3 Read this sentence from the story.

Police officers tried to keep the peace.

What does the word *peace* mean?

A. part

B. coin

C. calmness

D. agreement

Read this sentence.

She read aloud the school motto that was chiseled in stone.

What does *chiseled* mean?

F. shown

G. carved

H. spelled

I. painted

5 The setting of this story includes all of the following details EXCEPT

A. the inside of a classroom.

B. the month, day, and year.

C. a description of the weather.

D. the state where it takes place.

6 Which phrase BEST describes Cathy's character?

F. shy and modest

G. angry and defiant

H. nervous and fearful

I. brave and confident

© Macmillan/McGraw-Hill

7 Which phrase BEST describes Tyrone's character?

   A. angry and loud

   B. calm and detached

   C. bold and outspoken

   D. nervous and cautious

8 Based on the question Cathy asks at end of the story, she MOST LIKELY

   F. prefers not to look back at the past.

   G. remains angry about what happened.

   H. does not like being asked for her autograph.

   I. does not realize the importance of what she did.

Go On ▶

9 Why do you think the protesters react the way they do when the African-American students go to the school? Include details and information from the story in your answer.

_____

_____

_____

_____

_____

_____

_____

_____

_____

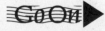

Student Name _____

Read and answer questions 10–12 on your Answer Sheet.

 Which word is spelled incorrectly?

A. nozzle

B. frightin

C. marvel

D. woolen

11 Read this sentence.

The <u>captan</u> gave a <u>chuckle</u> when she saw the <u>heron</u> on the <u>mountain</u>.

Which underlined word is spelled incorrectly?

F. heron

G. captan

H. chuckle

I. mountain

12 Read this sentence.

<u>Listen</u> to the <u>fable</u> about a golden <u>sandal</u> and a <u>barral</u> full of fish.

Which underlined word is spelled incorrectly?

A. fable

B. listen

C. barral

D. sandal

Below is a first draft of an autobiography that Celia wrote. The autobiography contains errors. Read the autobiography to answer questions 13–15.

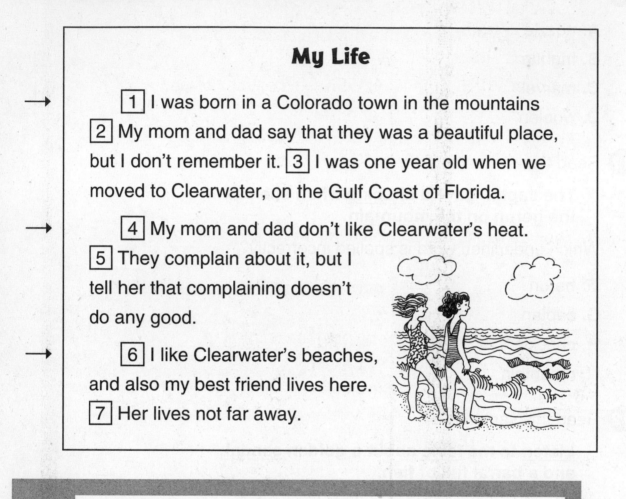

My Life

→ ⬛1 I was born in a Colorado town in the mountains ⬛2 My mom and dad say that they was a beautiful place, but I don't remember it. ⬛3 I was one year old when we moved to Clearwater, on the Gulf Coast of Florida.

→ ⬛4 My mom and dad don't like Clearwater's heat. ⬛5 They complain about it, but I tell her that complaining doesn't do any good.

→ ⬛6 I like Clearwater's beaches, and also my best friend lives here. ⬛7 Her lives not far away.

What do these mean?

⬛1   This type of symbol is in the Florida test to show a sentence number.

→   This symbol in the test shows a new paragraph.

The test may include the kinds of writing you might do. You will be asked to change and improve the writing.

Go On ▶

13 What is the correct way to write sentence 2?

    F. My mom and dad say that it was a beautiful place, but I don't remember it.

    G. My mom and dad say that it was a beautiful place, but I don't remember them.

    H. My mom and dad say that he was a beautiful place, but I don't remember it.

    I. My mom and dad say that he was a beautiful place, but I don't remember them.

14 What is the correct way to write sentence 5?

    A. They complain about it, but I tell they that complaining doesn't do any good.

    B. They complain about it, but I tell them that complaining doesn't do any good.

    C. They complain about them, but I tell her that complaining doesn't do any good.

    D. They complain about them, but I tell him that complaining doesn't do any good.

15 Which word should replace "Her" in sentence 7?

    F. It

    G. My

    H. She

    I. They

STOP

Student Name _____

Grade 5 • Unit 4 • Week 1
Student Evaluation Chart

Tested Skills	Number Correct	Percent Correct
Vocabulary Strategies: *Homophones, 1, 3; context clues, 2, 4*	/4	%
Reading Comprehension: *Plot development: character and setting, 5, 6, 7, 8*	/4	%
Short response: *Plot development: character and setting, 9*	/2	%
Spelling: *Final /əl/ and /ən/, 10, 11, 12*	/3	%
Grammar, Mechanics, and Usage: *Pronoun and antecedent agreement, 13, 14, 15*	/3	%
Total Weekly Test Score	**/16**	**%**

Correlations

Item	FCAT Assessed Benchmarks*	New Sunshine State Standards
1	LA.A.1.2.3	LA.5.1.6.8
2	LA.A.1.2.3	LA.5.1.6.3
3	LA.A.1.2.3	LA.5.1.6.8
4	LA.A.1.2.3	LA.5.1.6.3
5	LA.E.1.2.2	LA.5.2.1.2
6	LA.E.1.2.2	LA.5.2.1.2
7	LA.E.1.2.2	LA.5.2.1.2
8	LA.E.1.2.2	LA.5.2.1.2
9	LA.E.1.2.2	LA.5.2.1.2
10		LA.5.3.4.1
11		LA.5.3.4.1
12		LA.5.3.4.1
13		LA.5.3.4.5
14		LA.5.3.4.5
15		LA.5.3.4.5

* See benchmarks and standards on pages 379–384.

Name _____

Date _____

FCAT Format Weekly Assessment

TESTED SKILLS AND STRATEGIES

- **Vocabulary Strategies**
- **Reading Comprehension**
- **Spelling**
- **Grammar, Mechanics, and Usage**

Macmillan
McGraw-Hill

Read the story "A Good Defense" before answering Numbers 1 through 9.

A Good Defense

It was a cool Saturday morning when Vicente left his house wearing a warm jacket and sweat pants. He hiked to one of the deep arroyos outside his small New Mexico town. Even though he had lived there all his life, he never got tired of the beauty of the arroyos. In summer, the season of sudden storms, these ditches flowed with water. Now it was nearly November, and the bed of the arroyo just ahead of him was dry.

Outdoors was usually a calm, soothing place for a person to reflect. But Vicente's thoughts were far from calm at that moment. He was thinking about the bully who had chased him from the schoolyard on Friday afternoon. Even worse, he was thinking about how he had fled like a jackrabbit from the older, stronger boy. His face burned at the unpleasant memory. He didn't want to be a coward. Cowardly behavior wasn't acceptable—not when you had a father who had seen combat in two wars.

Go On ▶

Vicente sat down at the edge of the arroyo, where chamisa, skunkbush, and Apache plume grew freely. The cooling breeze felt good on his face. The moist banks offered a secluded home for the small animals that hid from predators. Snakes, ground squirrels, and rabbits nestled in the shelter of the soft soil bed of the arroyo. Vicente gazed at a jackrabbit nibbling the tall grasses. Suddenly, the scene in the schoolyard played again in his head. He fought a sinking sensation: a jackrabbit—that's what *he* was.

A shadow momentarily blanketed the sky. Vicente glanced up to see a large hawk wheeling overhead. It hung in the sky an instant, and Vicente realized that the raptor had gotten a glimpse of the jackrabbit. The jackrabbit froze to avoid arousing the hawk's attention. Some animals defended themselves this way, while others turned to fight.

Go On ▶

The hawk cruised lower in the sky and then hovered. "Little jackrabbit, if you don't want to be the hawk's meal, you'd better move fast," Vicente thought. But the brown creature seemed stunned by the nearness of the hawk and remained motionless. So the two animals had recognized each other: hunter and hunted.

As the bird swooped even lower, Vicente could hesitate no longer. He grabbed a small stone and flung it toward the jackrabbit. When the stone landed inches from the animal, it made a desperate leap for denser cover in the underbrush. Vicente looked up. The hawk linger a moment longer and then glided away.

"Good for you, jackrabbit," Vicente thought. "You escaped your foe." He had to acknowledge that sometimes it simply was wiser to run from trouble.

Student Name _____

**Now answer Numbers 1 through 9 on your Answer Sheet.
Base your answers on the story "A Good Defense."**

1 Read these sentences from the story.

> **Even though he had lived there all his life, he never got tired of the beauty of the arroyos. In summer, the season of sudden storms, these ditches flowed with water.**

Which word in the sentences helps you understand the meaning of *arroyos*?

A. beauty

B. storms

C. season

D. ditches

2 Read this sentence from the story.

> **Cowardly behavior wasn't acceptable—not when you had a father who had seen combat in two wars.**

Which word means almost the SAME as *behavior*?

F. words

G. actions

H. thinking

I. movement

3 Read this sentence from the story.

> **The moist banks offered a secluded home for the small animals that hid from predators.**

Which word means almost the SAME as *secluded*?

A. open

B. grassy

C. hidden

D. crowded

Go On ▶

Read this sentence from the story.

Snakes, ground squirrels, and rabbits nestled in the shelter of the soft soil bed of the arroyo.

Which word in the sentence helps you understand the meaning of *nestled*?

F. soil

G. arroyo

H. shelter

I. ground

5 Read this sentence.

The jackrabbit seemed stunned by the appearance of the hawk and was too shocked to move.

Which word in the sentence helps you understand the meaning of *stunned*?

A. move

B. hawk

C. shocked

D. appearance

6 At the beginning of the story, why does the author state that Vicente was "thinking about how he had fled like a jackrabbit from the older, stronger boy"?

F. to point out that rabbits are timid creatures

G. to show that Vicente knows he is a fast runner

H. to suggest that Vicente is like a rabbit in many ways

I. to show that Vicente feels troubled by what he had done

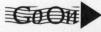

© Macmillan/McGraw-Hill

7 The author MOST LIKELY has the hawk hunt for the jackrabbit to show that

    A. the hawk is a magnificent bird of prey.

    B. the jackrabbit is a foolish, fearful animal.

    C. many animals must hide or run from predators.

    D. life in the arroyo is dangerous for small creatures.

8 The author PROBABLY wrote this story to

    F. explain how animals find shelter in an arroyo.

    G. teach readers about the hunting habits of hawks.

    H. entertain readers with a story about nature's rules.

    I. persuade readers that New Mexico is a beautiful place.

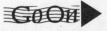

9 Why did the author MOST LIKELY call this story "A Good Defense"? Include details and information from the story in your answer.

_____

_____

_____

_____

_____

_____

_____

_____

_____

GoOn ▶

Student Name _____

Read and answer questions 10–12 on your Answer Sheet.

10 Which word is spelled incorrectly?

    A. fauset

    B. coward

    C. laundry

    D. applause

11 Read this sentence.

> The child stayed within the <u>boundary</u> her parents had set: her manners were <u>flawless</u>, she used <u>caution</u> when eating, and she did not act <u>roudy</u>.

Which underlined word is spelled incorrectly?

    F. roudy

    G. caution

    H. flawless

    I. boundary

12 Read this sentence.

> The <u>lawyur</u> was <u>grouchy</u> because his <u>trousers</u> got wet in the summer <u>shower</u>.

Which underlined word is spelled incorrectly?

    A. lawyur

    B. shower

    C. grouchy

    D. trousers

Student Name _____

Read and answer questions 13–15 on your Answer Sheet.

13 Read the sentence in the box.

> **She accepted the flowers graciously and then gave them to him to hold.**

Which word below is the **subject pronoun** in the sentence in the box?

F. She

G. him

H. them

14 Read the sentence in the box.

> **We waved to them on the way to our seats.**

Which word below is the **object pronoun** in the sentence in the box?

A. We

B. our

C. them

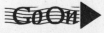

15 In which sentence below are all **pronouns** correct?

    F. Nan took the dog shampoo and handed her to Lia.

    G. Lia carefully put those on they wet dog, Jelly Bean.

    H. Jelly Bean barked because he wasn't happy
       with them.

STOP

Grade 5 • Unit 4 • Week 2
Student Evaluation Chart

Tested Skills	Number Correct	Percent Correct
Vocabulary Strategies: *Context clues: clues within sentences,* 1, 4, 5; *synonyms,* 2, 3	/5	%
Reading Comprehension: *Author's purpose,* 6, 7, 8	/3	%
Short response: *Author's purpose,* 9	/2	%
Spelling: *More accented syllables,* 10, 11, 12	/3	%
Grammar, Mechanics, and Usage: *Subject and object pronouns,* 13, 14; *proper use of subject and object pronouns,* 15	/3	%

Total Weekly Test Score	/16	%

Correlations

Item	FCAT Assessed Benchmarks*	New Sunshine State Standards
1	LA.A.1.2.3	LA.5.1.6.3
2	LA.A.1.2.3	LA.5.1.6.8
3	LA.A.1.2.3	LA.5.1.6.8
4	LA.A.1.2.3	LA.5.1.6.3
5	LA.A.1.2.3	LA.5.1.6.3
6	LA.A.2.2.2	LA.5.1.7.2
7	LA.A.2.2.2	LA.5.1.7.2
8	LA.A.2.2.2	LA.5.1.7.2
9	LA.A.2.2.2	LA.5.1.7.2
10		LA.5.3.4.1
11		LA.5.3.4.1
12		LA.5.3.4.1
13		LA.5.3.4.4
14		LA.5.3.4.4
15		LA.5.3.4.4

* See benchmarks and standards on pages 379–384.

FLORIDA
Treasures

Name _____

Date _____

FCAT Format Weekly Assessment

TESTED SKILLS AND STRATEGIES

- **Vocabulary Strategies**
- **Reading Comprehension**
- **Spelling**
- **Grammar, Mechanics, and Usage**

Mc Graw Hill **Macmillan McGraw-Hill**

Read the article "Democracy in the United States" before answering Numbers 1 through 9.

Democracy in the United States

The United States is a democracy. The word *democracy* comes from two Greek words: *demos*, which means "people," and *kratos*, which means "power" or "strength." In a democracy the citizens of a country elect their leaders. In the United States, the president and the members of the Senate and the House of Representatives are elected to office.

Not all countries of the world are democracies. In some countries, rulers are compelled to lead. They have no other choice because they are born into a ruling family. The United States has never had a ruling family. In other countries, a ruler may take over the government by force. This has never happened in the United States, either.

The United States federal government has three parts, called "branches." The *legislative branch* is made up of the Senate and the House of Representatives. Together these two government bodies are called the United States Congress. The main job of Congress is to legislate, that is, to create laws. Members of Congress also have the power to mint money, control taxes, and declare war. The citizens of each state elect two senators, no matter how many inhabitants live in that state. However, the number of representatives who will represent a state in Congress depends on the state's population. The greater the population is, the greater the number of elected representatives it has.

State	Population in 2000	Number of Representatives	Number of Senators
California	33,930,798	53	2
Florida	16,028,890	25	2
Michigan	9,995,829	15	2
Vermont	609,890	1	2

Representation in the House is based on a state's population.

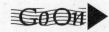

The president leads the branch of government that carries out the laws. This branch is called the *executive branch*, and it includes the people the president selects to help him or her and to head government offices. Leading the armed forces is another presidential duty.

The third branch of government, the *judicial branch*, is the country's court system. The judicial branch interprets, or explains, the laws and determines when people are being disrespectful by breaking them. This branch is headed by the Supreme Court. The Supreme Court is made up of nine justices who decide how the laws of the Constitution apply to specific situations. Unlike the members of the other branches of government, Supreme Court justices are not elected. They are appointed by the president and can serve on the Court for life.

Each branch of the federal government can check the actions of the other two branches. This balances the branches' actions and helps to make each branch act fairly. Under this system, it is difficult for one part of the government to gain too much power.

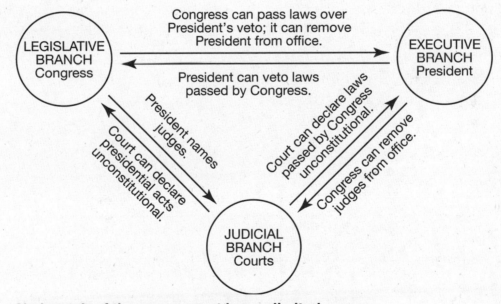

No branch of the government has unlimited power.

~Go On▶

For a democracy to succeed, the people of the country must participate. Without enough participation, a democracy will fail. In the United States, citizens may register to vote when they reach 18 years of age. However, some people take on this responsibility unenthusiastically. They are absorbed in other interests and are too preoccupied to participate in the government at all. In some elections, less than 50 percent of registered voters take advantage of their right to vote!

Student Name _____

Now answer Numbers 1 through 9 on your Answer Sheet.
Base your answers on the article "Democracy in the
United States."

1 Read these sentences from the article.

> **In some countries, rulers are compelled to lead.
> They have no other choice because they are born
> into a ruling family.**

What does *compelled* mean?

A. asked   **C.** elected

B. forced   **D.** chosen

2 Read this sentence from the article.

> **The judicial branch interprets, or explains,
> the laws and determines when people are being
> disrespectful by breaking them.**

What does *disrespectful* mean?

F. full of respect   **H.** respected again

G. lacking respect   **I.** respected before

3 Read these sentences from the article.

> **For a democracy to succeed, the people of
> the country must participate. Without enough
> participation, a democracy will fail.**

What does *succeed* mean?

A. get started

B. establish itself

C. continue forever

D. turn out as planned

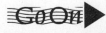

4 Read this sentence from the article.

However, some people take on this responsibility unenthusiastically.

The prefix and suffix help you understand that the word *unenthusiastically* means

F. excited again.

G. excited before.

H. full of excitement.

I. lacking excitement.

5 Read this sentence from the article.

They are absorbed in other interests and are too preoccupied to participate in the government at all.

What does *preoccupied* mean in the sentence?

A. bored

B. forgetful

C. prepared

D. distracted

6 Which statement below applies to all three branches of the federal government?

F. All of their members are elected.

G. They do not have unlimited power.

H. Their members are appointed for life.

I. Their size is based on state population.

Student Name _____

7 The caption under the diagram is MOST relevant to which idea discussed in the article?

    A. the president's duties

    B. the participation of citizens

    C. the system of checks and balances

    D. the election of the president and members of Congress

8 Which statement from the article is LEAST important for understanding its subject?

    F. "The United States federal government has three parts, called 'branches.'"

    G. "For a democracy to succeed, the people of the country must participate."

    H. "The judicial branch interprets, or explains, the laws and determines when people are being disrespectful by breaking them."

    I. "The word *democracy* comes from two Greek words: *demos*, which means 'people,' and *kratos*, which means 'power' or 'strength.'"

Go On ▶

9 "A democracy is the most effective form of government."
Use details and information from the article to:

READ
THINK
EXPLAIN

- explain what this generalization means, and

- support your explanation

_____

_____

_____

_____

_____

_____

_____

_____

_____

_____

_____

_____

_____

_____

_____

_____

_____

_____

GoOn ▶

Student Name _____

Read and answer questions 10–12 on your Answer Sheet.

10 Which word is spelled incorrectly?

A. extract

B. content

C. subjekt

D. entrance

11 Read this sentence.

The <u>rebal</u> will <u>protest</u> the rules and <u>refuse</u> to enter the <u>contest</u>.

Which underlined word is spelled incorrectly?

F. rebal

G. refuse

H. protest

I. contest

12 Read this sentence.

People need <u>permitts</u> to camp in the <u>desert</u>, even if they plan to <u>conduct</u> <u>research</u> rather than take a vacation.

Which underlined word is spelled incorrectly?

A. desert

B. conduct

C. permitts

D. research

Read the instructions titled "How to Make a Smiling Pizza." Choose the word that correctly completes questions 13 and 14.

How to Make a Smiling Pizza

Most kids <u>(13)</u> making food that's fun. Here's how to make a smiling pizza!

Step 1: Cook a cheese pizza.

Step 2: Wash two cherry tomatoes. Cut 2 long and 4 short carrot sticks. Cut three medium-length strips of red bell pepper.

Step 3: When the pizza <u>(14)</u> cooled off, put the vegetables on it to make a face. Use the tomatoes for eyes, the 2 long carrot sticks for the nose, 2 short carrot sticks for each eyebrow, and the strips of bell pepper for the smiling mouth.

Step 4: Enjoy your smiling pizza!

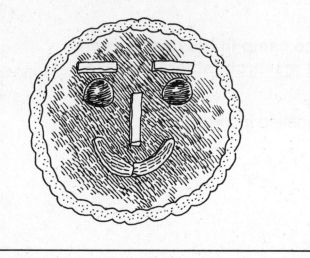

13 Which answer should go in blank (13)?

  F. enjoy

  G. enjoys

  H. enjoying

14 Which answer should go in blank (14)?

  A. is

  B. be

  C. are

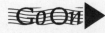

Student Name _____

Read and answer question 15 on your Answer Sheet.

15 In which sentence below is all **punctuation** correct?

   F. Dr Samuels greeted Ben Ebert with a smile.

   G. She wrote the date, Feb 28, 2007, on his chart.

   H. His next appointment would be on Thurs., March 10.

STOP

Grade 5 • Unit 4 • Week 3

Student Evaluation Chart

Tested Skills	Number Correct	Percent Correct
Vocabulary Strategies: *Context clues,*1, 3, 5; *prefixes and suffixes,* 2, 4	/5	%
Reading Comprehension: *Relevant facts and details,* 6, 7, 8	/3	%
Extended response: *Relevant facts and details,* 9	/4	%
Spelling: *Accented syllables in homographs,* 10, 11, 12	/3	%
Grammar, Mechanics, and Usage: *Pronoun-verb agreement,* 13, 14; *use correct abbreviations,* 15	/3	%

Total Weekly Test Score	/18	%

Correlations

Item	FCAT Assessed Benchmarks*	New Sunshine State Standards
1	LA.A.1.2.3	LA.5.1.6.3
2	LA.A.1.2.3	LA.5.1.6.7
3	LA.A.1.2.3	LA.5.1.6.3
4	LA.A.1.2.3	LA.5.1.6.7
5	LA.A.1.2.3	LA.5.1.6.3
6	LA.A.2.2.1	LA.5.2.2.2
7	LA.A.2.2.1	LA.5.2.2.2
8	LA.A.2.2.1	LA.5.2.2.2
9	LA.A.2.2.1	LA.5.2.2.2
10		LA.5.3.4.1
11		LA.5.3.4.1
12		LA.5.3.4.1
13		LA.5.3.4.5
14		LA.5.3.4.5
15		LA.5.3.4.3

* See benchmarks and standards on pages 379–384.

Name _____

Date _____

FCAT Format Weekly Assessment

TESTED SKILLS AND STRATEGIES

- Vocabulary Strategies
- Reading Comprehension
- Spelling
- Grammar, Mechanics, and Usage

Macmillan
McGraw-Hill

Read the article "The Life of a Hurricane" before answering Numbers 1 through 9.

The Life of a Hurricane

What do hurricanes, cyclones, and typhoons have in common? They all are different names for the same severe tropical storm that is known as a *tropical cyclone*. In this article, the word *hurricane* will be used to discuss this type of storm.

What causes a hurricane to develop over ocean water? At least three elements must be present. First, the water must be warm enough to give off heat and moisture into the atmosphere. Second, evaporated water already available in the air must mix with the heat and moisture rising from the ocean. Finally, easterly winds must be present. The wind moves the heat and evaporated water high into the atmosphere. Then the Earth's rotation begins to work against the easterly winds. This twists the growing storm into a cylinder. The center of this cylinder is called the *eye*.

When the heat and moisture from the ocean's surface come into contact with the cooler air higher up, thunderstorms develop. Then the cooler air travels back toward the ocean's surface and pulls more moisture from the ocean. Once that moisture rises into the thunderclouds, it is released as torrential rain. This type of rain usually accompanies hurricanes. The winds increase in speed and begin to move the enormous storm across the ocean. As long as hurricanes remain over water, they can keep increasing in size and strength.

Go On ▶

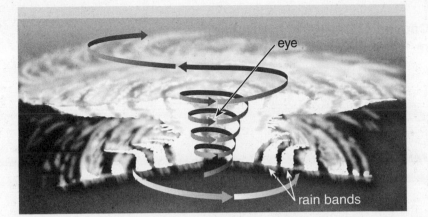

Usually the weather is calm in eye of the hurricane, which may range from 2 miles to 200 miles in diameter. Rain bands spiral toward the center of the hurricane, often bringing high winds and heavy rainfall; calmer weather is found between each rain band.

What causes the storm to end? Sometimes a hurricane dies when it travels into the path of strong westerly winds. This disturbs its course and may cause the storm to travel over cooler northern waters. Without the energy from the evaporated ocean water, the storm finally loses power and dies out. At other times, a hurricane travels until it hits land. Once it is over land, it causes enormous damage. Tornadoes may form in the rain bands. High winds knock over structures. The ocean surge floods towns and also causes extensive destruction of property. But without the warm ocean water as an energy source, a hurricane over land also loses power. Eventually, it ends up as rain showers.

Go On ▶

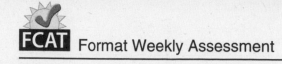
**Leading Causes of Deaths in the United States
from Tropical Cyclones, 1970–1999**

Freshwater
Flooding
59%

Wind 12%

Surf 11%

Offshore 11%

Tornado 4%

Other 2%

Surge 1%

Hurricanes can be very destructive forces.

However, hurricanes are not all bad. A few of their effects
actually are positive. They bring needed rain to regions that usually
are dry. For example, hurricanes in the eastern north Pacific Ocean
can relieve drought conditions in the southwestern United States
and in northern Mexico. Hurricanes also positively affect the
global balance of heat. That is, they move warm, moist air from
tropical regions northward. As a result, the heat in these regions
becomes less intense.

© Macmillan/McGraw–Hill

Student Name _____

**Now answer Numbers 1 through 9 on your Answer Sheet.
Base your answers on the article "The Life of a Hurricane."**

1 Read this sentence from the article.

> **First, the water must be warm enough to give off
> heat and moisture into the atmosphere.**

What does the word *atmosphere* mean?

A. air   **C.** mood

B. land   **D.** feeling

2 Read this sentence from the article.

> **When the heat and moisture from the ocean's
> surface come into contact with the cooler air higher
> up, thunderstorms develop.**

What does *contact* mean in the sentence?

F. person

G. joining

H. messenger

I. communication

3 Read this sentence.

> **High winds can result in the destruction of buildings.**

What does the word *destruction* mean in the sentence?

A. storm   **C.** damage

B. injuries   **D.** flooding

4 Read this sentence.

Flooding from hurricanes causes extensive property damage in towns near the ocean.

Which word means about the SAME as *property*?

F. hope

G. ownership

H. confidence

I. possessions

5 What does the caption under the first diagram describe?

A. the parts of a hurricane

B. the effects of a hurricane

C. the steps in a hurricane's development

D. the elements that must be present for a hurricane to form

6 What must be present BEFORE a hurricane develops?

F. Wind, cool ocean water, and land

G. Warm ocean water, wind, and rain

H. Moisture in the air, wind, and cool ocean water

I. Warm ocean water, moisture in the air, and wind

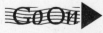

7 What happens RIGHT AFTER heat and moisture from the ocean's surface mix with cooler air?

    A. The hurricane dies out.

    B. Thunderstorms develop.

    C. The storm moves across the ocean.

    D. The storm takes on the shape of a cylinder.

8 What technique does the author MAINLY use to present information about hurricanes?

    F. describing a process

    G. problem and solution

    H. compare and contrast

    I. advantages and disadvantages

Go On ▶

9 How does the author organize the details in the second, third, and fourth paragraphs of "The Life of a Hurricane"? Explain your answer using information from the article.

READ
THINK
EXPLAIN

_____

_____

_____

_____

_____

_____

_____

_____

_____

_____

_____

_____

_____

_____

_____

Go On ▶

Student Name _____

Read and answer questions 10–12 on your Answer Sheet.

10 Which word is spelled incorrectly?

   A. butchur

   B. treasure

   C. moisture

   D. stretcher

11 Read this sentence.

> The <u>ranchur</u> gave a <u>lecture</u> on the <u>pleasure</u> of working in <u>nature</u>.

Which underlined word is spelled incorrectly?

   F. nature

   G. lecture

   H. ranchur

   I. pleasure

12 Read this sentence.

> The artist had to <u>meazure</u> the <u>mixture</u> carefully to create <u>azure</u> paint that matched the color of the flowers in the <u>pasture</u>.

Which underlined word is spelled incorrectly?

   A. azure

   B. mixture

   C. pasture

   D. meazure

Student Name _____

Read and answer questions 13–15 on your Answer Sheet.

13 Read the sentence in the box.

> The committee asked for her help with field day, and she agreed to time the races.

Which word in the sentence in the box is a **possessive pronoun**?

F. to

G. her

H. she

14 Which sentence below contains a **possessive pronoun**?

A. Karen wants us to help her sell the lemonade she made.

B. The judges said that of all the models mine was the best.

C. We don't know the answer, and we can't help you find it.

15 In which sentence below is all **punctuation** correct?

    F. The blue gray sky clouded over this afternoon.

    G. A hot-air balloon race was taking place twenty-one miles away.

    H. The citizens were grateful for their town's new firstclass, under-ground shelter.

Grade 5 · Unit 4 · Week 4
Student Evaluation Chart

Tested Skills	Number Correct	Percent Correct
Vocabulary Strategies: *Multiple-meaning words, 1, 2; context clues, 3; synonyms, 4*	/5	%
Reading Comprehension: *Recognize organizational patterns: description, 6, 7, 8*	/3	%
Extended response: *Recognize organizational patterns: description, 9*	/4	%
Spelling: *Words with /chər/ and /zhər/, 10, 11, 12*	/3	%
Grammar, Mechanics, and Usage: *Possessive pronouns, 13, 14; use hyphens, 15*	/3	%

Total Weekly Test Score	/18	%

Correlations

Item	FCAT Assessed Benchmarks*	New Sunshine State Standards
1	LA.A.1.2.3	LA.5.1.6.9
2	LA.A.1.2.3	LA.5.1.6.9
3	LA.A.1.2.3	LA.5.1.6.3
4	LA.A.1.2.3	LA.5.1.6.8
5	LA.A.1.2.3	LA.5.1.6.3
6	LA.A.2.2.7	LA.5.1.7.5
7	LA.A.2.2.7	LA.5.1.7.5
8	LA.A.2.2.7	LA.5.1.7.5
9	LA.A.2.2.7	LA.5.1.7.5
10		LA.5.3.4.1
11		LA.5.3.4.1
12		LA.5.3.4.1
13		LA.5.3.4.4
14		LA.5.3.4.4
15		LA.5.3.4.3

* See benchmarks and standards on pages 379–384.

Name _____

Date _____

FCAT Format Weekly Assessment

TESTED SKILLS AND STRATEGIES

- Vocabulary Strategies
- Reading Comprehension
- Spelling
- Grammar, Mechanics, and Usage

Macmillan
McGraw-Hill

Read the story "Raven the Trickster and Fish Hawk" before answering Numbers 1 through 9.

Raven the Trickster and Fish Hawk: A Retelling of a Native American Tale

Raven was a Trickster. He was always fooling others to get what he wanted. One day, the bird called Fish Hawk was unfortunate enough to happen upon Raven on the riverbank. Before he could fly away, Raven spotted him.

"Ah, my dearest friend," Raven greeted Fish Hawk. "The weather has turned cold and bitter. Let us go to your house and warm ourselves."

Fish Hawk was too polite to refuse. But it was without enthusiasm that he led Raven to his home. Once inside, Raven glanced about slyly and noticed that the hawk had laid in a large supply of food. Fish Hawk also had made his home quite comfortable with drinking gourds and soft blankets of leaves and grasses.

© Macmillan/McGraw–Hill

"What a lot of merchandise you have here," sneaky Raven said. "You could open your own store! You would need a treasurer to collect the profit on these wares!"

When Fish Hawk said nothing in response, Raven continued. "And, besides, I know how much you pride yourself on keeping a clean and tidy home. That requires a lot of time and effort! Why don't I visit with you during the winter months, and we can share some of the burdens of housekeeping?"

Fish Hawk doubted the wisdom of this plan, but he let Raven stay with him. It soon became clear that Raven would not lift a feather to help his kind host. In time, Fish Hawk grew tired of his lazy guest. But Raven talked to him sweetly, saying, "Don't worry, dear friend. This beach will be covered with fish, and you will not have to catch them. I'll get our dinner for us while you rest."

Go On ▶

Poor Fish Hawk decided to give Raven another chance. Yet weeks passed by and Raven did nothing to help. He made his host gather food for both of them while he slept and ate up the meals. Thanking Fish Hawk many times after each large dinner, he would say, "What a rich, wise friend you are! I have so much appreciation for your kindness. Words can hardly express my feelings." He would always conclude this speech by again assuring Fish Hawk that he would catch fish. But, of course, nothing came of this empty promise.

Fish Hawk finally grew dismayed and disgusted by Raven's laziness and greed, and he flew away from his own house. "That will educate you, Raven!" he called out. "Now you will have to fend for yourself!" He hoped to teach Raven a lesson. Yet, deep in his heart, he knew that the old Trickster would never change.

Fish Hawk soon built himself a cozy new home. And Raven had to find his own dinner from then on.

GoOn ▶

Student Name _____

Now answer Numbers 1 through 9 on your Answer Sheet.
Base your answers on the story "Raven the Trickster and
Fish Hawk."

1 Read this sentence from the story.

> **One day, the bird called Fish Hawk was unfortunate
> enough to happen upon Raven on the riverbank.**

Unlucky is to *unfortunate* as *happy* is to

A. glad.

B. smile.

C. frown.

D. unhappy.

2 Read these sentences from the story.

> **"What a lot of merchandise you have here," sneaky
> Raven said. "You could open your own store!"**

Merchandise is to *products* as *store* is to

F. shop.

G. prices.

H. products.

I. shoppers.

3 Read this sentence from the story.

> **"Why don't I visit with you during the winter
> months, and we can share some of the burdens of
> housekeeping?"**

Which word means about the SAME as *burdens*?

A. steps   **C.** duties

B. hours   **D.** details

GoOn ▶

© Macmillan/McGraw–Hill

4 Read this sentence from the story.

> "I have so much appreciation for your kindness."

Which word means about the SAME as *appreciation*?

F. jealousy

G. enjoyment

H. thankfulness

I. understanding

5 Read these sentences from the story.

> "That will educate you, Raven!" he called out.
> "Now you will have to fend for yourself!"

Which word means about the SAME as *educate*?

A. bore

B. teach

C. scare

D. learn

6 Why does the author state that "Raven glanced about slyly" at Fish Hawk's home?

F. to show that Raven has keen eyesight

G. to suggest that Raven is a polite creature

H. to show that Raven admires Fish Hawk's house

I. to suggest that Raven is about to play a trick on Fish Hawk

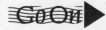

© Macmillan/McGraw-Hill

7 The author MOST LIKELY has Raven thank Fish Hawk
many times to show that Raven

   A. is very grateful

   B. is a hard worker

   C. wants to anger Fish Hawk

   D. is very skillful at tricking others

8 The author PROBABLY wrote this story to

   F. inform readers about trickster tales.

   G. persuade readers to learn more about trickster tales.

   H. instruct readers with a trickster tale about dishonesty.

   I. let readers know why Raven is a well-known figure in
trickster tales.

Go On ▶

9 Why does the author have Fish Hawk leave his own home at the end of the story? Use details and information from the story to support your answer.

READ
THINK
EXPLAIN

_____

_____

_____

_____

_____

_____

_____

_____

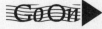

Student Name _____

Read and answer questions 10–12 on your Answer Sheet.

10 Which word is spelled incorrectly?

   A. substence

   B. resistance

   C. persistence

   D. disturbance

11 Read this sentence.

> **The <u>performance</u> was marked by the <u>brilliance</u> and <u>radiance</u> of the dancers, not by the <u>absance</u> of the director.**

Which underlined word is spelled incorrectly?

   F. radiance

   G. absance

   H. brilliance

   I. performance

12 Read this sentence.

> **The patient needed <u>assistance</u> into the <u>ambulence</u> because his <u>balance</u> was poor and he could walk only a short <u>distance</u>.**

Which underlined word is spelled incorrectly?

   A. balance

   B. distance

   C. assistance

   D. ambulence

Go On ▶

The movie review below is a first draft that Miryam wrote for her teacher. The review contains errors. Read the movie review to answer questions 13–15.

A Very Funny Movie

→ [1] Would you like to see a really funny movie?

[2] Then I advise you to go see *The Tale of a Dog's Tail*.

[3] Its the funniest movie I've seen in a long time.

→ [4] The movie is about two sisters and theyr dog Poochie. [5] Something mysterious causes Poochie's tail to keep growing and growing.

[6] His unusual tail causes all kinds of problems!

→ [7] Your going to love this movie, and you'll be happy you listened to my advice.

What do these mean?

[1] This type of symbol is in the Florida test to show a sentence number.

→ This symbol in the test shows a new paragraph.

The test may include the kinds of writing you might do. You will be asked to change and improve the writing.

© Macmillan/McGraw–Hill

Go On ▶

13 What is the correct way to write sentence 3 ?

    F. Its the funniest movie Ive seen in a long time.

    G. It's the funniest movie I've seen in a long time.

    H. Its' the funniest movie I've seen in a long time.

    I. It has the funniest movie I've seen in a long time.

14 Which word should replace "theyr" in sentence 4 ?

    A. their

    B. there

    C. theyre

    D. they're

15 What is the correct way to write sentence 7 ?

    F. Youre going to love this movie, and youll be happy you listened to my advice.

    G. You're going to love this movie, and youll be happy you listened to my advice.

    H. You're going to love this movie, and you'll be happy you listened to my advice.

    I. Your'e going to love this movie, and you'll be happy you listened to my advice.

STOP

Student Name _____

Grade 5 • Unit 4 • Week • 5
Student Evaluation Chart

Tested Skills	Number Correct	Percent Correct
Vocabulary Strategies: *Analogies: relationships,* 1, 2; *synonyms,* 3, 4, 5	/5	%
Reading Comprehension: *Author's purpose,* 6, 7, 8	/3	%
Short response: *Author's purpose,* 9	/2	%
Spelling: *Words with* –ance *and* -ence, 10, 11, 12	/3	%
Grammar, Mechanics, and Usage: *Apostrophes and possessives,* 13; *pronouns, contractions, and homophones,* 14, 15	/3	%

Total Weekly Test Score	/16	%

Correlations

Item	FCAT Assessed Benchmarks*	New Sunshine State Standards
1	LA.A.1.2.3	LA.5.1.6.3
2	LA.A.1.2.3	LA.5.1.6.3
3	LA.A.1.2.3	LA.5.1.6.8
4	LA.A.1.2.3	LA.5.1.6.8
5	LA.A.1.2.3	LA.5.1.6.8
6	LA.A.2.2.2	LA.5.1.7.2
7	LA.A.2.2.2	LA.5.1.7.2
8	LA.A.2.2.2	LA.5.1.7.2
9	LA.A.2.2.2	LA.5.1.7.2
10		LA.5.3.4.1
11		LA.5.3.4.1
12		LA.5.3.4.1
13		LA.5.3.4.3
14		LA.5.3.4.3
15		LA.5.3.4.3

* See benchmarks and standards on pages 379–384.

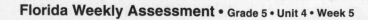

Name _____

Date _____

FCAT Format Weekly Assessment

TESTED SKILLS AND STRATEGIES

- **Vocabulary Strategies**
- **Reading Comprehension**
- **Spelling**
- **Grammar, Mechanics, and Usage**

Macmillan McGraw-Hill

Read the article "Roald Amundsen, Polar Explorer" before answering Numbers 1 through 9.

Roald Amundsen, Polar Explorer

Roald Amundsen was a famous polar explorer. In 1897 Amundsen joined an expedition that made scientific investigations in Antarctica. In 1903 he became the first European to travel the Northwest Passage.

Amundsen had dreamed of being the first European to reach the North Pole, but Robert E. Peary got there first. As a result, Amundsen abandoned the idea of an expedition to the North Pole and began planning one to the South Pole instead. He kept this plan secret because he did not want Robert Falcon Scott's team to know what he was doing. Scott also was planning an expedition to the South Pole, and Amundsen did not want him to know that he had competition.

Amundsen's ship, the *Fram,* left Norway on August 9, 1910, eight weeks after the departure of Scott's team. On board were 97 Greenland sled dogs. Amundsen believed that sled dogs would be more effective than the ponies and tractors with motors that Scott used to pull his sledges. The *Fram* also carried a hut and enough supplies to last the crew for two years. The supplies included lamps, food, tools, and medicines for the treatment of injuries.

Four months later, the *Fram* reached the Ross Ice Shelf. The men built their base camp at the Bay of Whales. Because the team members would need supplies and shelter along the route to the South Pole, they set

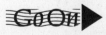

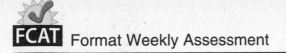
up depots, or storage places for supplies, along the way. The labor was difficult and demanding, and the men had to finish their tasks as fast as they could. They were in a race against time. The long, dark nights of winter would begin in April. Amundsen also worried about Scott's team reaching the South Pole before him.

On September 8, the team of eight men started off over the treacherous ice with sledges that were pulled by 86 dogs. One man stayed behind to watch over their base camp. Frigid weather set in, so the team made a run for the nearest depot. The weather was so bad that the team had to return to the base camp. As soon as the weather improved, a smaller group started

Go On ▶

out again. Amundsen and four other men struggled through blizzards and over glaciers. They were determined to beat Scott's expedition, despite the delay that the terrible weather had caused.

Finally, on December 14, 1911, Amundsen and his men reached the uninhabited South Pole. The team members planted the Norwegian flag in the frozen ground to celebrate their victory over Scott and the harsh conditions they had endured along the way.

Go On ▶

Student Name _____

Now answer Numbers 1 through 9 on your Answer Sheet. Base your answers on the article "Roald Amundsen, Polar Explorer."

1 Read this sentence from the article.

> **In 1897 Amundsen joined an expedition that made scientific investigations in Antarctica.**

What does the word *expedition* mean?

A. decision

B. experiment

C. trip made for pleasure

D. trip made for a purpose

2 Read this sentence from the article.

> **As a result, Amundsen abandoned the idea of an expedition to the North Pole and began planning one to the South Pole instead.**

What does *abandoned* mean?

F. escaped

G. ignored

H. gave up

I. left behind

3 Read this sentence from the article.

> **The labor was difficult and demanding, and the men had to finish their tasks as fast as they could.**

Which word means almost the SAME as *labor*?

A. work

B. route

C. camp

D. weather

Go On

4 Which word from the article has a suffix that means "act of"?

   F. supplies

   G. explorer

   H. treatment

   I. treacherous

5 Read this sentence from the article.

   Finally, on December 14, 1911, Amundsen and his men reached the uninhabited South Pole.

The prefix *-un* tells you that *uninhabited* means

   A. not lived in.

   B. not close by.

   C. not interesting.

   D. not in the habit of.

6 What problem did Roald Amundsen face in his exploration of the South Pole?

   F. He could not keep his plans for the expedition a secret.

   G. He was unable to find eight experienced men for his team.

   H. He did not take enough supplies for the trip across the Arctic.

   I. He was worried that he would not be the first person to reach the South Pole.

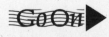

7 What helped Amundsen succeed in reaching the South Pole BEFORE Scott?

    A. building a base camp

    B. starting the trip before Scott

    C. getting help from Scott's team

    D. using sled dogs for transportation

8 What problem did Amundsen and his team face in September 1911?

    F. Robert E. Peary reached the North Pole.

    G. The long, dark nights made travel impossible.

    H. Very cold weather slowed down the team's progress.

    I. Setting up the base camp involved a great deal of work.

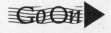

9 Why did Amundsen and his team set up depots between their base camp and their destination? Use information and details from the article to support your answer.

READ
THINK
EXPLAIN

_____

_____

_____

_____

_____

_____

_____

_____

_____

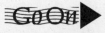

Student Name _____

Read and answer questions 10–12 on your Answer Sheet.

 Which word is spelled incorrectly?

    A. surge

    B. margin

    C. legend

    D. knowlege

 Read this sentence.

> The park <u>ranjer</u> did not want to <u>plunge</u> over the <u>ridge</u>, so she had to <u>dodge</u> the tangled branches.

Which underlined word is spelled incorrectly?

    F. ridge

    G. dodge

    H. ranjer

    I. plunge

12 Read this sentence.

> The <u>ajent</u> tried to pick up the <u>baggage</u> and carry it into the <u>lodge</u>, but it was too heavy to <u>budge</u>.

Which underlined word is spelled incorrectly?

    A. ajent

    B. lodge

    C. budge

    D. baggage

Go On

Student Name _____

Read and answer questions 13–15 on your Answer Sheet.

13 Read the sentence in the box.

> **Please bring me the <u>heavy</u> <u>sweater</u> that <u>hangs</u> in my closet.**

Which underlined word in the sentence in the box is used as an **adjective**?

F. heavy

G. hangs

H. sweater

14 Which sentence below uses a **demonstrative adjective**?

A. "What do you think of that?" Lee asked his mother.

B. Kendra gave her mom that blue vase for her birthday.

C. The new owner said he is happy that people like his shop.

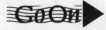

15 In which sentence below is all **capitalization** correct?

    F. Which colors are in the Mexican Flag?

    G. They studied Asian and African elephants.

    H. The woman in the small Japanese car is a Doctor.

STOP

Student Name _____

Grade 5 • Unit 5 • Week 1
Student Evaluation Chart

Tested Skills	Number Correct	Percent Correct
Vocabulary Strategies: *Context clues, 1, 2; synonyms, 3; base and root words with affixes, 4, 5*	/5	%
Reading Comprehension: *Problem and solution,* 6, 7, 8	/3	%
Short response: *Problem and solution,* 9	/2	%
Spelling: *Words with soft* g, 10, 11, 12	/3	%
Grammar, Mechanics, and Usage: *Adjectives and demonstrative adjectives,* 13, 14; *capitalize proper adjectives,* 15	/3	%

Total Weekly Test Score	**/16**	**%**

Correlations

Item	FCAT Assessed Benchmarks*	New Sunshine State Standards
1	LA.A.1.2.3	LA.5.1.6.3
2	LA.A.1.2.3	LA.5.1.6.3
3	LA.A.1.2.3	LA.5.1.6.8
4	LA.A.1.2.3	LA.5.1.6.7
5	LA.A.1.2.3	LA.5.1.6.7
6	LA.E.1.2.2	LA.5.2.1.2
7	LA.E.1.2.2	LA.5.2.1.2
8	LA.E.1.2.2	LA.5.2.1.2
9	LA.E.1.2.2	LA.5.2.1.2
10		LA.5.3.4.1
11		LA.5.3.4.1
12		LA.5.3.4.1
13		LA.5.3.4.4
14		LA.5.3.4.4
15		LA.5.3.4.2

* See benchmarks and standards on pages 379–384.

FLORIDA
Treasures

Name _____

Date _____

FCAT Format Weekly Assessment

TESTED SKILLS AND STRATEGIES

- **Vocabulary Strategies**
- **Reading Comprehension**
- **Spelling**
- **Grammar, Mechanics, and Usage**

Mc Graw Hill **Macmillan
McGraw-Hill**

Read the story "A Matter of Taste" before answering Numbers 1 through 9.

A Matter of Taste

Some people claimed that Claudia's grandmother was a superb cook. They even said that she could have been a professional chef in a fancy restaurant. But she preferred cooking for family and friends. Grandma Gillian would set a table with bubbling stews, braided breads, and vegetables simmered in spicy sauces. And her desserts were divine. Whenever she came to visit, Claudia's house began to smell quite interesting.

"You should experience foods from other countries, dear," Grandma Gillian informed her. "You can realize the tastes of people all over the world reflected in the foods they create. Every civilization has some wonderful foods to offer."

But Claudia would eat only a limited number of foods—mainly hot dogs, macaroni and cheese, pizza, and hamburgers. She turned up her nose at her grandmother's dishes, with their complex sauces made of many ingredients. She refused to sample those weird foods. Her grandmother never complained about it. She simply threw a hamburger onto the grill. Claudia wondered whether this was part of a strategy to get her to try new foods.

© Macmillan/McGraw–Hill

Go On

One night Claudia had an unusual experience. The night started out normally enough. Claudia did her homework, ate a hamburger for dinner, read for a while, and went to sleep. But later she seemed to have floated out of her bed and circled the globe. When she landed, she was in China—at least, that is where she thought she was. A girl took her by the hand and led her to her home, where a feast was in progress. People passed Claudia dishes of hot dumplings, steamed fish, and pork. This array smelled delicious, and there was no shortage of food. But as she lifted the chopsticks holding a dumpling to her lips, she began to float again. She hadn't been able to taste even one morsel of the food.

Next she descended into a desert, where travelers on camels hailed her and invited her to dine with them. A pot of chickpeas and rice simmered in their tent. The travelers' traditional flat breads were given to the diners, and a stew was ladled onto each one. How incredible the food smelled! But, once again, Claudia never got even a single bite. Suddenly she was floating over the earth, her stomach empty. She felt like an outcast.

Go On ▶

The next day Claudia was exhausted. Her room resembled bedlam, with the pillows tossed off the bed and the blankets all knotted up. Still in her pajamas, she went downstairs to the fragrant-smelling kitchen. She sniffed and asked, "Grandma, what's that wonderful aroma?"

The stew pot bubbled merrily, and Grandma Gillian beamed.

GoOn ▶

Student Name _____

**Now answer Numbers 1 through 9 on your Answer Sheet.
Base your answers on the story "A Matter of Taste."**

1 Read this sentence from the story.

> **"You can realize the tastes of people all over the
> world reflected in the foods they create."**

What does *reflected* mean?

A. pictured

B. reviewed

C. reminded

D. represented

2 Read this sentence from the story.

> **She turned up her nose at her grandmother's dishes,
> with their complex sauces made of many ingredients.**

The word *complex* comes from a Latin word that means
"to embrace or include." What does *complex* mean in
the sentence?

F. coming together

G. cooking with spices

H. twisting and turning

I. containing many things

3 Read this sentence from the story.

> **Claudia wondered whether this was part of a strategy
> to get her to try new foods.**

The word *strategy* comes from a Greek word that means
"the act of a general." What does *strategy* mean?

A. plan

B. trick

C. excuse

D. thought

Go On ▶

© Macmillan/McGraw–Hill

4 Read this sentence from the story.

> **The travelers' traditional flat breads were given to the diners, and a stew was ladled onto each one.**

What is the BEST meaning for the word *traditional*?

  F. unique

  G. out-of-date

  H. passed down

  I. old-fashioned

5 Read this sentence from the story.

> **Her room resembled bedlam, with the pillows tossed off the bed and the blankets all knotted up.**

Bedlam was the popular name for a London hospital for the mentally ill. What does the word *bedlam* mean?

  A. a type of bed

  B. a distant country

  C. a state of confusion

  D. a strange new flavor

6 Which question BEST helps to identify the theme of the first two paragraphs of the story?

  F. How did Grandma Gillian learn to cook?

  G. Why do people find different foods tasty?

  H. What can be learned from trying new foods?

  I. Why do some people prefer to cook only for family and friends?

7 What is an important theme in this story?

   A. Stick to the foods you know and like.

   B. Too much imagination can get a person into trouble.

   C. You can experience a different culture by trying its foods.

   D. Always be polite to older people who are visiting your home.

8 Which title BEST expresses the essential message of this story?

   F. "The Magic Kettle"

   G. "The World in a Dish"

   H. "Claudia's Nightmare"

   I. "Grandma Gillian's Visit"

9 What essential message about life does the story "A Matter of Taste" give the reader? Use details and information from the story to support your answer.

READ
THINK
EXPLAIN

_____

_____

_____

_____

_____

_____

_____

_____

_____

_____

_____

_____

_____

_____

_____

_____

_____

_____

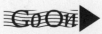

Student Name _____

Read and answer questions 10–12 on your Answer Sheet.

10 Read this sentence.

> **The guests stayed in a beautiful <u>maner</u> house,
> in the <u>suite</u> by the <u>pier</u>, where they could hear the
> boats' bells <u>peal</u>.**

Which underlined word is spelled incorrectly?

A. pier

B. peal

C. suite

D. maner

11 Read this sentence.

> **Her <u>presentce</u> included a <u>stationary</u> bike, a box
> of <u>stationery</u> for writing letters, and a box of
> <u>sweet</u> oranges.**

Which underlined word is spelled incorrectly?

F. sweet

G. presentce

H. stationary

I. stationery

12 Which word is spelled incorrectly?

A. peel

B. waist

C. waste

D. curent

Read and answer questions 13–15 on your Answer Sheet.

( ) Read the sentence in the box.

> **Today students <u>will</u> read <u>an</u> essay they are sure <u>to</u> enjoy.**

Which underlined word in the sentence in the box is an **article**?

F. an

G. to

H. will

( ) In which sentence below are all **articles** correct?

A. Let's go see an new movie tonight.

B. We can share a bag of popcorn at the movie.

C. The movie stars a only child and her two dogs.

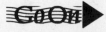

Student Name _____

15 Read the lines from a play in the box.

> **1** HARRY; Are you sure you really saw him?
>
> **2** JANE: *(Wringing her hands.)* Yes. He was at the station buying a bus ticket.
>
> **3** HARRY. *(Whistling low.)* What are we going to do now, Jane?

In which line in the box is all **punctuation** correct?

F. line **1**

G. line **2**

H. line **3**

STOP

Florida Weekly Assessment • Grade 5 • Unit 5 • Week 2   271   11

Student Name _____

Grade 5 • Unit 5 • Week 2
Student Evaluation Chart

Tested Skills	Number Correct	Percent Correct
Vocabulary Strategies: *Context clues,* 1, 4; *word origins,* 2, 3, 5	/5	%
Reading Comprehension: *Essential message/theme,* 6, 7, 8	/3	%
Extended response: *Essential message/theme,* 9	/4	%
Spelling: *Homophones,* 10, 11, 12	/3	%
Grammar, Mechanics, and Usage: *Articles,* 13, 14; *use a colon,* 15	/3	%
Total Weekly Test Score	**/18**	%

Correlations

Item	FCAT Assessed Benchmarks*	New Sunshine State Standards
1	LA.A.1.2.3	LA.5.1.6.3
2		LA.5.1.6.11
3		LA.5.1.6.11
4	LA.A.1.2.3	LA.5.1.6.3
5		LA.5.1.6.1
6	LA.A.2.2.1	LA.5.1.7.3
7	LA.A.2.2.1	LA.5.1.7.3
8	LA.A.2.2.1	LA.5.1.7.3
9	LA.A.2.2.1	LA.5.1.7.3
10		LA.5.3.4.1
11		LA.5.3.4.1
12		LA.5.3.4.1
13		LA.5.3.4.4
14		LA.5.3.4.4
15		LA.5.3.4.3

* See benchmarks and standards on pages 379–384.

Name _____

Date _____

FCAT Format Weekly Assessment

TESTED SKILLS AND STRATEGIES

- • **Vocabulary Strategies**
- • **Reading Comprehension**
- • **Spelling**
- • **Grammar, Mechanics, and Usage**

Mc Graw Hill **Macmillan McGraw-Hill**

Read the article "Animal Communities" before answering Numbers 1 through 9.

Animal Communities

In human communities, people work together. Working together helps us to obtain food and shelter, raise children, and enjoy a higher quality of life. When each person contributes to a community, the community functions better. A society needs many different kinds of workers in order to thrive.

Animals also live in diverse and varied communities. In fact, nature instills most creatures with a social instinct that serves a number of purposes.

Many lions work together in well-organized groups. The females do the hunting. They work as a team to trap their prey. Because of this, the lions can surround an animal and cut off its escape. Wolves also hunt in teams. They have a strong social order. They follow a leader and obey rules for the good of the pack.

Lions are social animals who work together in groups, called prides.

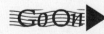

The members of bee, ant, and wasp communities have special jobs. For instance, a queen and various types of workers live in a bee hive. The worker bees serve the queen. As a result, the queen lays eggs. If the queen did not lay enough eggs, the busy hive would soon become vacant. In an ant community, soldier ants protect the colony. In bee and wasp communities, females take on the job of providing protection.

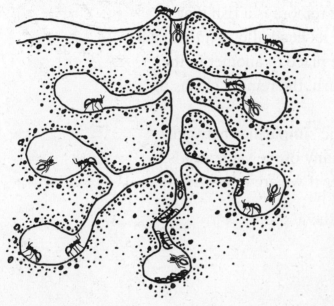

Ants live together in nests made up of many tunnels and chambers. As they move through the tunnels, they may communicate with each other by tapping with their sensitive antennae.

Naturalist Dr. Regis Ferriere notes that some insect species exist cooperatively. An example is the relationship between ants and aphids. The ants watch over groups of aphids on grasses as if they were herds of cattle. From time to time the ants "milk" the aphids of sugar droplets. In turn, the ants protect the aphids from predators.

Go On ▶

Baboons and antelopes often eat together to protect one another. Because the baboons have excellent eyesight and the antelope have a keen sense of smell, together they function as a warning system. Cattle and birds work in much the same way. The birds eat the insects that the cattle stir up. In turn, the birds make a lot of noise and fly off if they sense danger. This warns the cattle. Thus, their combined efforts benefit both the birds and the cattle.

Another example of two very different animals helping each other can be found in warm oceans. The remora is a fish that cannot swim well. However, the form of its head allows it to attach itself to large sharks. So it gets from one place to another in the ocean by getting rides from sharks. In turn, the remora cleans the shark of small animals that hurt it.

As you can see, there are certain basic similarities between human and animal societies. We have many of the same needs, after all. We must depend on one another if we are to survive in a complex world.

Student Name _____

**Now answer Numbers 1 through 9 on your Answer Sheet.
Base your answers on the article "Animal Communities."**

1 Read this sentence from the article.

> **Animals also live in diverse and varied communities.**

Which word means the OPPOSITE of *diverse*?

A. alike   **C.** different

B. hostile   **D.** multiple

2 Read this sentence from the article.

> **If the queen did not lay enough eggs, the busy hive would soon become vacant.**

Which word means the OPPOSITE of *vacant*?

F. blank

G. empty

H. occupied

I. abandoned

3 Read this sentence from the article.

> **Naturalist Dr. Regis Ferriere notes that some insect species exist cooperatively.**

What would a *naturalist* MOST LIKELY study?

A. nature and natural history

B. things that happen naturally

C. projects that involve working with people

D. how people work naturally with each other

Go On ▶

4 Read this sentence from the article.

> **Thus, their combined efforts benefit both the birds and the cattle.**

Which word means the OPPOSITE of *combined*?

F. linked

G. related

H. attached

I. separated

5 Which statement below is NOT an effect of people living together in a cooperative community?

A. The community provides jobs for people.

B. The community protects people from harm.

C. The community makes it safer to raise children.

D. The community provides free housing for everyone.

6 Why do ants tap their antennae?

F. to dig out dirt as they build tunnels

G. to find their way through dark tunnels

H. to communicate with other ants they encounter

I. to find out where to put the food they have carried

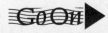

Student Name _____

7 When baboons and antelopes eat together, they

    A. are protected.

    B. eat the same food.

    C. develop similar habits.

    D. become natural enemies.

8 Which statement is an example of a cause and its effect?

    F. The cattle make noise, and the birds fly away.

    G. The cattle are predators, and the birds are hunted as prey.

    H. The cattle hunt the birds, which reduces the bird population.

    I. The cattle stir up the insects, which gives the birds more to eat.

Go On ▶

9 Describe a cause-and-effect relationship between animals that work together. Be sure to include details and information from the article.

READ
THINK
EXPLAIN

_____

_____

_____

_____

_____

_____

_____

_____

_____

_____

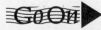

Student Name _____

Read and answer questions 10–12 on your Answer Sheet.

10 Which word is spelled incorrectly?

    A. preview

    B. disobey

    C. indefnite

    D. inexpensive

11 Read this sentence.

> **The jurors <u>missjudge</u> and <u>prejudge</u> the witnesses, leading to <u>mistaken</u> impressions and <u>injustice</u>.**

Which underlined word is spelled incorrectly?

    F. injustice

    G. prejudge

    H. mistaken

    I. missjudge

12 Read this sentence.

> **She <u>preheats</u> the oven while they <u>prewash</u> the stained clothes, and because they <u>misunderstand</u> the directions, they <u>desconnect</u> the television.**

Which underlined word is spelled incorrectly?

    A. prewash

    B. preheats

    C. desconnect

    D. misunderstand

GoOn ▶

The report below is a first draft that Elisabeth wrote for her teacher. Read the report to answer questions 13–15.

A Report from Africa

→ ⃞1 Mr. Lara works for the Lowry park zoo, and he told our class about his trip to Africa to study Elephants.

→ ⃞2 He said that elephants feel safest when they are all together. ⃞3 He showed us a photo of a large elephant and two small elephants. ⃞4 He said that the largest female elephant was the leader. ⃞5 He said the small elephants were her two calves, and the biggest one was older. ⃞6 He also said that the older calf was best at taking care of itself than the younger one was.

What do these mean?

⃞1   This type of symbol is in the Florida test to show a sentence number.

→   This symbol in the test shows a new paragraph.

The test may include the kinds of writing you might do. You will be asked to change and improve the writing.

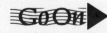

13 What is the correct way to write sentence ⬛1⬛?

    F. Mr. lara works for the Lowry park zoo, and he told our class about his trip to Africa to study elephants.

    G. Mr. Lara works for the Lowry Park Zoo, and he told our class about his trip to Africa to study elephants.

    H. Mr. Lara works for the Lowry Park zoo, and he told our class about his trip to africa to study Elephants.

    I. Mr. Lara works for the Lowry Park Zoo, and he told our class about his trip to Africa to study Elephants.

14 What is the correct way to write sentence ⬛5⬛?

    A. He said the small elephants were her two calves, and the big one was oldest.

    B. He said the small elephants were her two calves, and the bigger one was older.

    C. He said the small elephants were her two calves, and the biggest one was the older.

    D. He said the small elephants were her two calves, and the biggest one was the oldest.

15 What is the correct way to write sentence ⬛6⬛?

    F. He also said that the older calf was better at taking care of itself than the younger one was.

    G. He also said that the more old calf was best at taking care of itself than the more young one was.

    H. He also said that the older calf was more good at taking care of itself than the younger one was.

    I. He also said that the older calf was more better at taking care of itself than the youngest one was.

STOP

Grade 5 • Unit 5 • Week 3
Student Evaluation Chart

Tested Skills	Number Correct	Percent Correct
Vocabulary Strategies: *Antonyms*, 1, 2, 4; *context clues*, 3	/4	%
Reading Comprehension: *Cause and effect*, 5, 6, 7, 8	/4	%
Short response: *Cause and effect*, 9	/2	%
Spelling: *Prefixes* dis-, in-, mis-, pre-, 10, 11, 12	/3	%
Grammar, Mechanics, and Usage: *Review capitalization*, 13; *adjectives that compare*, 14, 15	/3	%

Total Weekly Test Score	/16	%

Correlations

Item	FCAT Assessed Benchmarks*	New Sunshine State Standards
1	LA.A.1.2.3	LA.5.1.6.8
2	LA.A.1.2.3	LA.5.1.6.8
3	LA.A.1.2.3	LA.5.1.6.3
4	LA.A.1.2.3	LA.5.1.6.8
5	LA.E.2.2.1	LA.5.1.7.4
6	LA.E.2.2.1	LA.5.1.7.4
7	LA.E.2.2.1	LA.5.1.7.4
8	LA.E.2.2.1	LA.5.1.7.4
9	LA.E.2.2.1	LA.5.1.7.4
10		LA.5.3.4.1
11		LA.5.3.4.1
12		LA.5.3.4.1
13		LA.5.3.4.2
14		LA.5.3.4.4
15		LA.5.3.4.4

* See benchmarks and standards on pages 379–384.

Name _____

Date _____

FCAT Format Weekly Assessment

TESTED SKILLS AND STRATEGIES

- **Vocabulary Strategies**
- **Reading Comprehension**
- **Spelling**
- **Grammar, Mechanics, and Usage**

Mc Graw Hill **Macmillan McGraw-Hill**

Read the story "To Honor a Hero" before answering Numbers 1 through 9.

To Honor a Hero

Martin sat quietly between his mother and his grandfather. The meeting hall was crowded with people who had come to pay their respects to a hero. Martin was confused. When he thought of heroes, people in action movies came to mind. He searched the creased, smiling faces of many of the elderly people sitting around him. But none of them looked much like a hero to him.

The speaker started his speech. "Friends, we are here to honor a man who served the Navajo people and the United States of America. This was a man who enlisted in the Marines during World War II. He signed up as a Navajo Code Talker."

The speaker looked around the audience. "Some of our youngsters may not know that many Navajo took part with the Marines in every battle in the Pacific Corridor from 1942 to 1945. Our men served in more than one invasion, and they were a crucial part of these attacks." Martin's eyes wandered over the faces of the older men. *Did some of them really play such an important role in a war?* he asked himself in disbelief.

Martin's shoulders sagged with boredom. He had heard about World War II in school. It belonged to the past. What was so exciting about a war, anyway? People were always fighting. Even on reservation land, where everyone lived and worked, people sometimes fought with each other.

Go On ▶

Martin turned his attention again to the speaker. "The time has come," the man was saying, "to honor our Code Talkers, now that so many of them have passed on. These were the people who helped assure victory in the war by sending and receiving coded messages about troop actions and orders. They sent vital information about each battle location so the Allies could position themselves at the site of the action. No member of the enemy Axis forces could break the Navajo Code during the Battle of Iwo Jima, and six of our people worked without sleep until that battle was won."

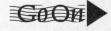

There were murmurs among the crowd, and Martin leaned forward. This was getting more interesting. "A man we know only as a friend and neighbor was a Code Talker," said the speaker. "After the war, he came home to help his people on the reservation. He did not forget his home, and so he will not be forgotten."

Then a surprising thing happened. The speaker asked Martin's grandfather to rise. "Let us honor one of our Code Talkers."

Martin glanced at his mom. There were tears in her eyes. He felt a tightening in his chest as he looked up at the man he thought he knew so well. His own grandfather—a hero!

**Now answer Numbers 1 through 9 on your Answer Sheet.
Base your answers on the story "To Honor a Hero."**

1 Read this sentence from the story.

> **He searched the creased, smiling faces of many of
> the elderly people sitting around him.**

Which word helps you understand what *creased* means?

A. sitting

B. elderly

C. smiling

D. searched

2 Read this sentence from the story.

> **"This was a man who enlisted in the Marines during
> World War II."**

What does *enlisted* mean?

F. enrolled   **H.** spoke for

G. attracted   **I.** engineered

3 Read this sentence from the story.

> **"Our men served in more than one invasion, and
> they were a crucial part of these attacks."**

Which word helps you understand what *invasion* means?

A. part

B. crucial

C. served

D. attacks

GO ON ▶

4 Read this sentence from the story.

> **Even on reservation land, where everyone lived and worked, people sometimes fought with each other.**

What is the BEST meaning for the word *reservation*?

F. a military base

G. an awards ceremony

H. a team of code talkers

I. land set aside by the government

5 Read this sentence from the story.

> **"They sent vital information about each battle location so the Allies could position themselves at the site of the action."**

What does the word *location* mean?

A. code

B. place

C. result

D. station

6 The author believes that the Navajo Code Talkers

F. were braver than the Marines.

G. made important contributions to the war.

H. should have stayed home and not gone to war.

I. should have been honored sooner than they were.

7 The author wants the reader to understand that Martin's grandfather was

  A. a modest and heroic man.

  B. the best Code Talker of all.

  C. of limited importance to the Marines.

  D. not so good at code talking as others were.

8 With which statement below would the author MOST LIKELY agree?

  F. Martin was right to be proud of his grandfather.

  G. Martin was right to be bored by a war from the distant past.

  H. Martin's grandfather should have been ashamed of how Martin was acting.

  I. Martin's grandfather should have told everyone sooner that he had been a Code Talker.

9 The story "To Honor a Hero" includes background information about the Navajo Code Talkers. Use details from the story to explain:

READ
THINK
EXPLAIN

- how the author feels about the Navajo Code Talkers, and

- why the author has this point of view

_____

_____

_____

_____

_____

_____

_____

_____

_____

_____

_____

_____

_____

Go On ▶

Student Name _____

Read and answer questions 10–12 on your Answer Sheet.

10 Which word is spelled incorrectly?

   A. sadness

   B. fondness

   C. weakness

   D. emptyness

11 Read this sentence.

> **In the <u>stilness</u> of the seemingly <u>bottomless</u> ocean, many sea creatures swim with <u>effortless</u> and <u>fearless</u> movements.**

Which underlined word is spelled incorrectly?

   F. stilness

   G. fearless

   H. effortless

   I. bottomless

12 Read this sentence.

> **In the <u>motionless</u> <u>darkness</u> of the cave, the hikers could hear the <u>ceasless</u> drip of water and the <u>harmless</u> noise of bats.**

Which underlined word is spelled incorrectly?

   A. ceasless

   B. harmless

   C. darkness

   D. motionless

© Macmillan/McGraw–Hill

GoOn ▶

Read the article "Turn Off the TV!" Choose the word or words that correctly complete questions 13 and 14.

Turn Off the TV!

Twenty years ago, most American kids spent a lot less time watching TV than they do today. And many of those kids of 20 years ago were __(13)__ than most of today's kids. Is there a strong connection between these two facts?

Whether there's a connection or not, here's some advice: Turn off your TV more often! Do something creative. Move your body. Learn a new skill.

This is the __(14)__ advice I can give you.

13 Which answer should go in blank (13)?

F. activer

G. most active

H. more active

14 Which answer should go in blank (14)?

A. usefulest

B. most useful

C. more useful

GoOn ▶

Student Name _____

Read and answer question 15 on your Answer Sheet.

15 Which sentence below is NOT written correctly?

   F. The Navajo code was more hard to break than other codes.

   G. The Navajo code really was the most difficult code ever created.

   H. Using the Navajo code was the most important decision of the war.

STOP

Student Name _____

Grade 5 • Unit 5 • Week 4
Student Evaluation Chart

Tested Skills	Number Correct	Percent Correct
Vocabulary Strategies: *Context clues*, 1, 2, 3, 4, 5	/5	%
Reading Comprehension: *Author's point of view*, 6, 7, 8	/3	%
Extended response: *Author's point of view*, 9	/4	%
Spelling: *Suffixes* -less *and* -ness, 10, 11, 12	/3	%
Grammar, Mechanics, and Usage: *Comparing with* more *and* most, 13, 14, 15	/3	%
Total Weekly Test Score	**/18**	**%**

Correlations		
Item	FCAT Assessed Benchmarks*	New Sunshine State Standards
1	LA.A.1.2.3	LA.5.1.6.3
2	LA.A.1.2.3	LA.5.1.6.3
3	LA.A.1.2.3	LA.5.1.6.3
4	LA.A.1.2.3	LA.5.1.6.3
5	LA.A.1.2.3	LA.5.1.6.3
6	LA.A.2.2.2	LA.5.1.7.2
7	LA.A.2.2.2	LA.5.1.7.2
8	LA.A.2.2.2	LA.5.1.7.2
9	LA.A.2.2.2	LA.5.1.7.2
10		LA.5.3.4.1
11		LA.5.3.4.1
12		LA.5.3.4.1
13		LA.5.3.4.4
14		LA.5.3.4.4
15		LA.5.3.4.4

* See benchmarks and standards on pages 379–384.

Name _____

Date _____

FCAT Format Weekly Assessment

TESTED SKILLS AND STRATEGIES

- Vocabulary Strategies
- Reading Comprehension
- Spelling
- Grammar, Mechanics, and Usage

Macmillan McGraw-Hill

Read the story "Whale-Watching" before answering Numbers 1 through 9.

Whale-Watching

Anita's dream had finally come true. She was holding on to the rail of a boat that took tourists to watch whales. The gentle, huge animals had always fascinated her. Then, last fall, her aunt Rachel and cousin Zach had moved to Hawaii. They had invited Anita's family to visit them during Anita's winter break from school. Now they all were on a whale-watching tour boat.

A whale emerged from the water by hurling itself up to the surface. With two or three beats of its huge tail, it sailed into the air, and then it fell back into the water with a splash. For a few seconds, it lay sprawled on the ocean's surface. Then its gigantic tail slapped the water a few times. The noise could be heard for a long distance. People watching the attraction from a nearby boat clapped their hands in awe and glee. The whale's showy display had focused everyone's attention on the enormous creature.

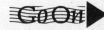

"Wow!" exclaimed Anita. "That was a humpback, wasn't it, Zach? I never dreamed an ocean animal could reach that size!"

Next to her, Anita's cousin Zach nodded wisely. "That one must have weighed 25 tons. But they can weigh even more, you know. Some humpbacks reach 30 tons."

A collective gasp from the crowd made Anita and Zach turn their attention to the opposite side of the tour boat. The two kids ventured over and were amazed to see another humpback surfacing right next to the vessel.

From earlier discussions with Zach, Anita knew that he wanted to be an oceanographer who specialized in whales. This led Anita to inquire, "What do oceanographers do?"

"Well," Zach replied, "they do all kinds of things related to the ocean. But I want to study whales in particular. Many species of whales are endangered, mostly because of human activity. I'd like to find ways to save them and increase their populations."

Anita looked at the majestic creature. She thought, *How odd that it's so close to us—members of the species that have brought it so much trouble.* She told Zach, "I think it's a great thing to do. These animals deserve all the help we can give them."

Zach nodded as he watched for more whales. "I'm glad you don't think it's unreasonable. It's going to take a lot of people like you and me working for many years to make a difference."

Go On

The sunshine warmed Anita, while the ocean breeze refreshed her. She looked at the cloudless sky and the dark blue water. She scanned the ocean from left to right and counted six single humpbacks and two pairs. *What a wonderful place to work,* she thought. At that moment she made a decision. As soon as she was home, she would do some research on whales and oceanographers. Maybe one day she and Zach would be working side by side.

Student Name _____

**Now answer Numbers 1 through 9 on your Answer Sheet.
Base your answers on the story "Whale-Watching."**

1 Read this sentence from the story.

> **A whale emerged from the water by hurling itself up to the surface.**

What does the word *emerged* mean?

A. dove

B. swam

C. floated

D. appeared

2 Read this sentence from the story.

> **The whale's showy display had focused everyone's attention on the enormous creature.**

Which word means about the SAME as *focused*?

F. outlined

G. pictured

H. discouraged

I. concentrated

3 Read this sentence from the story.

> **From earlier discussions with Zach, Anita knew that he wanted to be an oceanographer who specialized in whales.**

What does the word *discussions* mean?

A. talks

B. arguments

C. concerns

D. instructions

Go On ▶

4 Read this sentence from the story.

> **This led Anita to inquire, "What do oceanographers do?"**

The word *inquire* comes from a Latin word meaning "to seek." What does *inquire* mean in the sentence?

F. ask

G. draw

H. stare

I. move

5 Read this sentence from the story.

> **"I'm glad you don't think it's unreasonable."**

The word *unreasonable* has a Latin root that means "to think." What does *unreasonable* mean in the sentence?

A. think about

B. be thoughtful

C. without feeling

D. without thought

6 What is the BEST description of the setting of the story?

F. Hawaii when it is warm

G. the Pacific Ocean in December

H. a warm winter day on a boat in the ocean

I. a winter day where Anita's cousin Zach lives

© Macmillan/McGraw-Hill

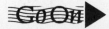

7 What does Anita learn from Zach?

    A. Only humpback whales are endangered.

    B. Humpbacks are the largest whale species.

    C. Some whale species are endangered due to the actions of humans.

    D. The sound of a whale's tail slapping can be heard for a long distance.

8 What is the LEAST LIKELY reason that Anita decides to research the profession of oceanographer when she gets home?

    F. her longtime interest in whales

    G. how content she feels on the boat

    H. the respect she has for her cousin

    I. what her cousin tells her about whales

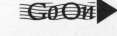

9 How is the setting of the story important to the plot of "Whale-Watching"? Explain your answer using details and information from the story.

READ
THINK
EXPLAIN

_____

_____

_____

_____

_____

_____

_____

_____

_____

_____

Go On ▶

Student Name _____

Read and answer questions 10–12 on your Answer Sheet.

10 Which word is spelled incorrectly?

  A. estimasion

  B. exhaustion

  C. impression

  D. concentration

11 Read this sentence.

> **The teachers <u>correct</u> the speeches and offer more <u>discussion</u> after school to help students <u>locate</u> the best candidates in the <u>electsion</u>.**

Which underlined word is spelled incorrectly?

  F. locate

  G. correct

  H. electsion

  I. discussion

12 Read this sentence.

> **Because of his <u>confusion</u> about the party's <u>location</u>, Ari could not <u>concentrate</u> on finding the <u>decorasions</u> he had promised to bring.**

Which underlined word is spelled incorrectly?

  A. location

  B. confusion

  C. concentrate

  D. decorasions

Read and answer questions 13–15 on your Answer Sheet.

13 Which sentence below is NOT written correctly?

   F. The weather is bad today, but it was worse yesterday.

   G. The food is good this week, but it was better last week.

   H. The marching band's performance was bad today, but it was best yesterday.

14 Which sentence below is NOT written correctly?

   A. Of those two artists, Palo is the better known.

   B. Christina plays the trumpet better than her twin sister Alexa.

   C. Kendall is less scared than I am, but Cory is the less scared of all of us.

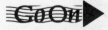

15 Read the sentence in the box.

> **This hurricane was bad, but the storm we had in 2005 was much worser.**

What is the correct way to write the sentence in the box?

F. This hurricanc was bad, but the storm we had in 2005 was much worse.

G. This hurricane was bad, but the storm we had in 2005 was more worser.

H. This hurricane was bad, but the storm we had in 2005 was much worster.

STOP

Student Name _____

Grade 5 • Unit 5
Student Evaluation Chart

Tested Skills	Number Correct	Percent Correct
Vocabulary Strategies: *Synonyms,* 1, 2, 3; *Latin roots,* 4, 5	/5	%
Reading Comprehension: *Plot development: character, setting,* 6, 7, 8	/3	%
Short response: *Plot development: setting, plot,* 9	/2	%
Spelling: *Adding* -ion, 10, 11, 12	/3	%
Grammar, Mechanics, and Usage: *Comparing* good *and* bad, 13, 15; *irregular comparative forms,* 14	/3	%

Total Weekly Test Score	/16	%

Correlations

Item	FCAT Assessed Benchmarks*	New Sunshine State Standards
1	LA.A.1.2.3	LA.5.1.6.8
2	LA.A.1.2.3	LA.5.1.6.8
3	LA.A.1.2.3	LA.5.1.6.8
4		LA.5.1.6.11
5		LA.5.1.6.11
6	LA.E.1.2.2	LA.5.2.1.2
7	LA.E.1.2.2	LA.5.2.1.2
8	LA.E.1.2.2	LA.5.2.1.2
9	LA.E.1.2.2	LA.5.2.1.2
10		LA.5.3.4.1
11		LA.5.3.4.1
12		LA.5.3.4.1
13		LA.5.3.4.4
14		LA.5.3.4.4
15		LA.5.3.4.4

* See benchmarks and standards on pages 379–384.

© Macmillan/McGraw–Hill

Name _____

Date _____

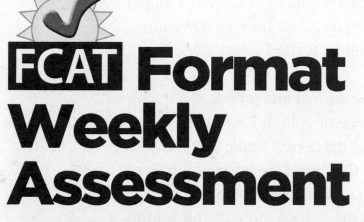

FCAT Format Weekly Assessment

TESTED SKILLS AND STRATEGIES

- **Vocabulary Strategies**
- **Reading Comprehension**
- **Spelling**
- **Grammar, Mechanics, and Usage**

Macmillan
McGraw-Hill

Read the story "Hans in Luck" before answering Numbers 1 through 9.

Hans in Luck: A Retelling of a Tale from the *Young Folks Treasury*

After seven years of hard work, Hans asked his master for his wages. The master gave Hans a big piece of gold. The young man took off for his village, anxious to see his mother after such a long absence. On the road, Hans met a man on a fine horse. The youth said, "How fortunate you are to be riding, while I weary myself trudging along."

The horseman descended from the animal and proposed a trade. "I'll trade you my stallion for that piece of gold in your hand."

When Hans agreed, the rider thrust the horse's bridle into the young man's hands. "Just utter 'C'ck! C'ck!' and the horse will gallop like lightning," he instructed and walked away. Of course, Hans immediately attempted to gallop. But the stallion instantly threw him off, and he landed in a ditch beside the road.

It was not long before a peasant woman happened to pass by, leading a cow. She was startled to see a young man in the ditch. Hans, rubbing a sore arm and leg, said to her, "I see you have a nice, quiet cow that no doubt gives refreshing milk. I'd rather your cow accompany me instead of this brute of a horse."

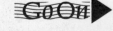

The peasant woman agreed to trade her cow for the horse. So Hans continued along the route to his village, driving the cow along and whistling merrily.

The day grew hot, and Hans grew thirsty. He tried to milk the cow. But he went about it in an awkward way, and the animal gave him a swift kick. Sweating, thirsty, and bruised, Hans was in great despair by this point.

Then along came a butcher driving a horse-drawn cart. In the cart was a huge pig. Hans told the butcher, "How I wish I had a pig. I'd have it butchered to make sausages and other delicacies."

"I'd be happy to trade you this prime pig for that worthless-looking cow," offered the butcher. The deal was quickly completed.

Go On ▶

Before twilight fell, Hans made even another trade: He swapped the pig for a goose. "My mother can use its soft feathers to stuff a pillow," he told himself.

Finally he entered his village. The first person he saw was a scissors-grinder at his trade. "Where did you get that goose?" the man asked Hans.

"I exchanged it for my pig," Hans replied, then worked backward to relate all his adventures to the scissors-grinder. When the man suggested that Hans trade the goose for his grinding stone, Hans consented.

But with each step Hans took, the stone seemed to grow heavier. Soon he laid it by the side of a stream that ran through the village. When he stooped to drink, the weighty stone tumbled into the water.

Free of any tiresome burdens now, Hans exclaimed, "I'm the luckiest man alive!" And he hastened homeward to his mother.

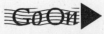

Student Name _____

**Now answer Numbers 1 through 9 on your Answer Sheet.
Base your answers on the story "Hans in Luck."**

1 Read this sentence from the story.

**The horseman descended from the animal and
proposed a trade.**

What does *descended* mean?

A. led to

B. got down

C. traded for

D. jumped away

2 Read this sentence from the story.

**When Hans agreed, the rider thrust the horse's
bridle into the young man's hands.**

What does *bridle* mean in the sentence?

F. to control   **H.** of a bride

G. a harness   **I.** a wedding

3 Read this sentence from the story.

**So Hans continued along the route to his village,
driving the cow along and whistling merrily.**

Which definition below describes a homophone for *route*?

A. *Noun.* a regular path

B. *Noun.* a traveled road

C. *Verb.* to give directions

D. *Noun.* the underground part of a plant

Go On ▶

Student Name _____

4 Read this sentence from the story.

Sweating, thirsty, and bruised, Hans was in great despair by this point.

Which word means almost the SAME as *despair*?

F. liveliness

G. joyfulness

H. greediness

I. hopelessness

5 Read this sentence from the story.

When the man suggested that Hans trade the goose for his grinding stone, Hans consented.

What does *consented* mean?

A. denied

B. agreed

C. refused

D. demanded

6 On Hans's journey home, which event happens FIRST?

F. Hans trades his cow for a pig.

G. A man rides by on a fine horse.

H. A horse flings Hans into a ditch.

I. Hans swaps his pig for a goose.

© Macmillan/McGraw-Hill

GoOn ▶

7 Which event happens AFTER Hans gets a pig?

    A. He attempts to milk a cow.

    B. He asks his master for his salary.

    C. He swaps his piece of gold for a horse.

    D. He trades a goose for a grinding stone.

8 Read the sentences in the box.

> **1. The horseman descends from the stallion.**
>
> **2. The peasant trades his cow for the horse.**
>
> **3. Hans meets a scissors-grinder in the village.**
>
> **4. Hans's master gives him a piece of gold.**

In what order do these events take place in the story?

    F. 1, 2, 4, 3

    G. 4, 3, 1, 2

    H. 4, 1, 2, 3

    I. 3, 1, 4, 2

9 What happens AFTER Hans trades the goose for the grinding stone? How does Hans feel about what happens? Use details and information from the story to support your answer.

_____

_____

_____

_____

_____

_____

_____

_____

Student Name _____

Read and answer questions 10–12 on your Answer Sheet.

10 Which word is spelled incorrectly?

A. fonics

B. disaster

C. mythical

D. astronomer

11 Which word is spelled incorrectly?

F. telegraph

G. mechanik

H. automatic

I. automobile

12 Read this sentence.

The children asked the <u>astranaut</u> to write her <u>autograph</u> on the <u>photograph</u> after they had seen her on <u>television</u>.

Which underlined word is spelled incorrectly?

A. television

B. astranaut

C. autograph

D. photograph

**Read the article "New Books of Fairy Tales Await Readers,"
which the librarian wrote for the school paper. Choose the
word or words that correctly complete questions 13 and 14.**

New Books of Fairy Tales Await Readers

There are several new books of fairy tales in our library. Come check them out, and then check out one to take home!

Don't think that fairy tales are just for little kids. They are for all ages—even adults! If they are written (13), they teach an important life lesson. And even if a fairy tale is written (14), it usually is still an entertaining story.

I hope to see you soon at the library. And remember to *keep reading*!

13 Which answer should go in blank (13)?

F. well

G. good

H. better

14 Which answer should go in blank (14)?

A. bad

B. worse

C. badly

Student Name _____

Read and answer question 15 on your Answer Sheet.

15 Read the sentence in the box.

> **The road was barely visible through the rain and fog.**

Which word in the sentence is used as an **adverb**?

F. barely

G. visible

H. through

STOP

Grade 5 • Unit 6 • Week 1
Student Evaluation Chart

Tested Skills	Number Correct	Percent Correct
Vocabulary Strategies: *Context clues,* 1, 4, 5; *homophones,* 2, 3	/5	%
Reading Comprehension: *Chronological order,* 6, 7, 8	/3	%
Short response: *Chronological order,* 9	/2	%
Spelling: *Greek roots,* 10, 11, 12	/3	%
Grammar, Mechanics, and Usage: *Using* good *and* well, 13; *adverbs,* 14, 15	/3	%
Total Weekly Test Score	**/16**	**%**

Correlations

Item	FCAT Assessed Benchmarks*	New Sunshine State Standards
1	LA.A.1.2.3	LA.5.1.6.3
2	LA.A.1.2.3	LA.5.1.6.8
3	LA.A.1.2.3	LA.5.1.6.8
4	LA.A.1.2.3	LA.5.1.6.3
5	LA.A.1.2.3	LA.5.1.6.3
6	LA.A.2.2.7	LA.5.1.7.5
7	LA.A.2.2.7	LA.5.1.7.5
8	LA.A.2.2.7	LA.5.1.7.5
9	LA.E.1.2.2	LA.5.2.1.2
10		LA.5.3.4.1
11		LA.5.3.4.1
12		LA.5.3.4.1
13		LA.5.3.4.4
14		LA.5.3.4.4
15		LA.5.3.4.4

* See benchmarks and standards on pages 379–384.

Name _____

Date _____

FCAT Format Weekly Assessment

TESTED SKILLS AND STRATEGIES

- **Vocabulary Strategies**
- **Reading Comprehension**
- **Spelling**
- **Grammar, Mechanics, and Usage**

Mc Graw Hill **Macmillan McGraw-Hill**

Read the story "Camping Out" before answering
Numbers 1 through 9.

Camping Out

"This tent was supposed to be really straightforward to put together," Randall told Nick as he scattered tent poles on the ground. "It was guaranteed to be uncomplicated enough for a child to set up. I'm in the fifth grade, and I guess you could still call me a child. But I can't figure it out." His voice was steadily getting louder. "My dad should demand our money back for this tent." He kicked one of the poles and yelled. "I'm really frustrated, and I'm going to tell my dad to let the manufacturer know about it!" He finished his speech by stomping the ground.

Randall, Nick, and their families were camping at a state park. The boys had convinced their parents to let them set up their own campsite a short distance from where everyone else would be. It was a clear October day. The leaves were beginning to turn gold and red, the sun was shining, and birds were chirping joyfully.

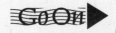

© Macmillan/McGraw-Hill

"Stop yanking on the cords," Nick suggested. "When my mom gets back from her hike, I'll ask her to supervise us. She's an expert at assembling tents. With her help we'll have our campsite set up in a flash."

Randall ignored Nick and continued to hurl parts of the tent around. Then he barked, "Where did I put that bundle? You know the one I need—it has all the cords and hooks inside it." He stormed around for a minute until he found the bag. But when he opened it he discovered that all the tape had melted. "This is the last straw!" he screamed. "All the tape has fused together." He threw down the bag and sat on the ground. "Why do people ever go camping? I should have stayed home and played video games. Even doing my math homework or cleaning my room would have been more fun than this."

"Relax, Randall," Nick said, sitting down beside his friend. "Look at the scenery. This time of year it's really impressive."

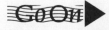

"Scenery?" Randall bellowed. "Trees and hills? Who wants to look at that stuff? And what's with all these bugs? This place is crawling with them." Suddenly the look on Randall's face softened a bit. His voice was much quieter when he said, "I don't feel at ease in nature. In fact, I feel tense and nervous."

"Gee, I never would have deduced that," said Nick with a slight smile. "Look. Here comes Mom. She can't do anything about the bugs. But she'll help us with the tent. Then next on the schedule is roasting hot dogs."

For the first time since they had arrived, Randall smiled. "Come to think of it," he said, "I'm starved."

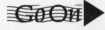

**Now answer Numbers 1 through 9 on your Answer Sheet.
Base your answers on the story "Camping Out."**

1 Read this sentence from the story.

> **"It was guaranteed to be uncomplicated enough for a child to set up."**

Which word means about the SAME as *guaranteed*?

A. sold

B. promised

C. packaged

D. assembled

2 Read this sentence from the story.

> **"When my mom gets back from her hike, I'll ask her to supervise us."**

What does the word *supervise* mean?

F. direct

G. ignore

H. relieve

I. abandon

3 Read this dictionary entry.

> **bun-dle** (bun´ d'l) **1.** *Noun.* a number of things wrapped together **2.** *Verb.* to wrap things together **3.** *Noun.* a considerable amount **4.** *Noun.* a group of muscle fibers

Which definition of *bundle* is used in the fourth paragraph of the story?

A. definition 1

B. definition 2

C. definition 3

D. definition 4

Go On ▶

4 Read this sentence from the story.

> **"All the tape has fused together."**

Which meaning of *fuse* is used in the sentence?

F. stitch

G. join by melting

H. a safety device

I. equip with a fuse

5 Which statement BEST describes Randall?

A. He is used to getting special attention.

B. He expects others to do things for him.

C. He adjusts well to unfamiliar situations.

D. He does not act very maturely for his age.

6 Which statement BEST describes Nick?

F. He is a kind, calm person.

G. He is shy and unsure of himself.

H. He is only somewhat cooperative.

I. He is similar to Randall in many ways.

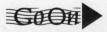

7 In the FIRST part of the story, Randall is

    A. hoping to go home soon.

    B. trying to hide what is bothering him.

    C. wishing that he and Nick were not friends.

    D. hoping Nick's mom will return soon from hiking.

8 Why does Randall MOST LIKELY have so much trouble putting the tent together?

    F. The tent is very difficult to put together.

    G. Randall does not have enough patience.

    H. Nick is not giving Randall enough help with the poles.

    I. The tent is defective and did not come with directions.

Go On ▶

9 Camping is a difficult experience for Randall. Use details and information from the story to explain:

READ
THINK
EXPLAIN

- why camping is a problem for Randall, and

- what he needs to do to be able to enjoy camping

_____
_____
_____
_____
_____
_____
_____
_____
_____
_____
_____
_____
_____
_____
_____
_____
_____
_____

© Macmillan/McGraw-Hill

GoOn ▶

Student Name _____

Read and answer questions 10–12 on your Answer Sheet.

10 Which word is spelled incorrectly?

    A. inspect

    B. respekt

    C. inspector

    D. transport

11 Which word is spelled incorrectly?

    F. distract

    G. attraction

    H. subtraction

    I. intermisson

12 Read this sentence.

> The <u>committee</u> arranged to <u>import</u> and <u>export</u> the <u>tracers</u>.

Which underlined word is spelled incorrectly?

    A. import

    B. export

    C. tracers

    D. committee

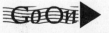

The story below is part of a first draft that Adele wrote for her teacher. The story contains errors. Read the story to answer questions 13–15.

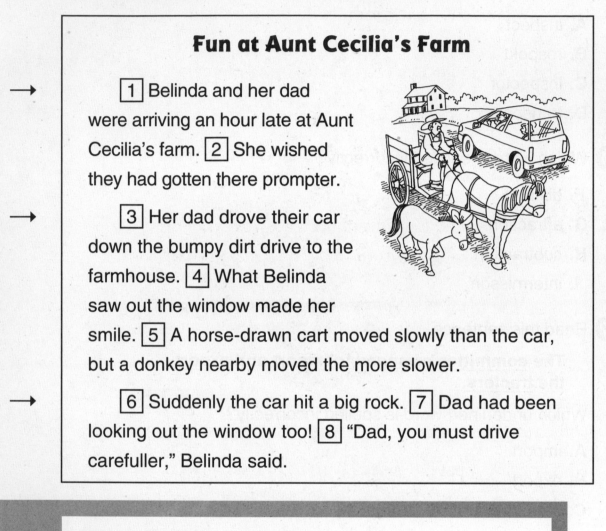

Fun at Aunt Cecilia's Farm

→ ⬚1⬚ Belinda and her dad were arriving an hour late at Aunt Cecilia's farm. ⬚2⬚ She wished they had gotten there prompter.

→ ⬚3⬚ Her dad drove their car down the bumpy dirt drive to the farmhouse. ⬚4⬚ What Belinda saw out the window made her smile. ⬚5⬚ A horse-drawn cart moved slowly than the car, but a donkey nearby moved the more slower.

→ ⬚6⬚ Suddenly the car hit a big rock. ⬚7⬚ Dad had been looking out the window too! ⬚8⬚ "Dad, you must drive carefuller," Belinda said.

What do these mean?

⬚1⬚ This type of symbol is in the Florida test to show a sentence number.

→ This symbol in the test shows a new paragraph.

The test may include the kinds of writing you might do. You will be asked to change and improve the writing.

Go On ▶

13 What is the BEST way to write sentence 2 ?

    F. She wished they had gotten there promptlier.

    G. She wished they had gotten there more prompt.

    H. She wished they had gotten there more promptly.

    I. She wished they had gotten there more prompter.

14 What is the BEST way to write sentence 5 ?

    A. A horse-drawn cart moved slow than the car, but a donkey nearby moved the slower.

    B. A horse-drawn cart moved slowly than the car, but a donkey nearby moved the slowest.

    C. A horse-drawn cart moved more slow than the car, but a donkey nearby moved the slowest.

    D. A horse-drawn cart moved more slowly than the car, but a donkey nearby moved the most slowly.

15 What is the BEST way to write 8 ?

    F. "Dad, you must drive more careful," Belinda said.

    G. "Dad, you must drive most carefully," Belinda said.

    H. "Dad, you must drive more carefully," Belinda said.

    I. "Dad, you must drive more carefuller," Belinda said.

STOP

Student Name _____

Grade 5 • Unit 6 • Week 2
Student Evaluation Chart

Tested Skills	Number Correct	Percent Correct
Vocabulary Strategies: *Context clues,* 1, 2, 5; *homophones,* 3, 4	/5	%
Reading Comprehension: *Plot development: make judgments,* 6, 7, 8	/3	%
Extended response: *Plot development: make judgments,* 9	/4	%
Spelling: *Latin roots,* 10, 11, 12	/3	%
Grammar, Mechanics, and Usage: *Adverbs that compare,* 13, 14; *using* more *and* most *without* -er *and* -est, 15	/3	%

Total Weekly Test Score	/18	%

Correlations

Item	FCAT Assessed Benchmarks*	New Sunshine State Standards
1	LA.A.1.2.3	LA.5.1.6.3
2	LA.A.1.2.3	LA.5.1.6.8
3	LA.A.1.2.3	LA.5.1.6.8
4	LA.A.1.2.3	LA.5.1.6.3
5	L.A.A.1.2.3	LA.5.1.6.3
6	L.A.E.1.2.2	LA.5.2.1.2
7	L.A.E.1.2.2	LA.5.2.1.2
8	L.A.E.1.2.2	LA.5.2.1.2
9	L.A.E.1.2.2	LA.5.2.1.2
10		LA.5.3.4.1
11		LA.5.3.4.1
12		LA.5.3.4.1
13		LA.5.3.4.4
14		LA.5.3.4.4
15		LA.5.3.4.4

* See benchmarks and standards on pages 379–384.

Name _____

Date _____

FCAT Format Weekly Assessment

TESTED SKILLS AND STRATEGIES

- **Vocabulary Strategies**
- **Reading Comprehension**
- **Spelling**
- **Grammar, Mechanics, and Usage**

Macmillan
McGraw-Hill

Read the article "Living Better, Thanks to Inventions!" before answering Numbers 1 through 9.

Living Better, Thanks to Inventions!

Inventions improve people's lives in many ways. Most people use inventions every day and never pause to consider who made them or how they were made. But life would be quite different without the many inventions we have come to rely on.

One of the most important inventions was the automobile. This invention forced people to improve roads and turn them from muddy gravel paths into paved highways. It led to the development of suburbs as more and more people moved out of large cities. In addition, the automobile helped people interact with each other by bringing them closer together. People could drive to their jobs or to their friends' and relatives' homes. The distance between places seemed to grow smaller with the arrival of the automobile.

Automobiles helped bring distant family members together.

Other inventions help fewer people, but they are no less important. The wheelchair, for example, assists people who cannot walk because of physical problems. A wheelchair is just that—a chair with wheels—although many of them also have motors. All wheelchairs are the same in one way: they all help physically challenged people get around. You may think that this invention will never be of use to you, but you cannot be sure. Anyone could fall and break a leg. A badly broken leg set in an inflexible, rigid plaster cast would keep you off your feet for months. You would be grateful then that the wheelchair had been invented. Nobody should ignore how valuable wheelchairs are.

The next time your telephone rings, express your gratitude to Alexander Graham Bell, the man who invented this device. Bell first tested his machine on March 10, 1876, and it quickly became popular. His initial invention opened up a whole new way of communicating. Imagine what life would be like without telephones. Almost everyone would find it nearly impossible!

The cellular phones so many people have today would never have been invented if it were not for Bell. Most people now think that cellular phones are a necessity of life.

Go On ▶

Today much of the work of transmitting phone calls—and thousands of other tasks—is done by computers. Computers are everywhere in the United States, and the country could not function without them. If computers were taken away, traffic would come to a halt. Businesses would close their doors. Lights would go out, and mayhem would ensue. Monica Johns, the successful president of a major company, has called the computer "an indispensable tool in today's economy."

Because these inventions are so familiar to us and we use them every day, they may seem simple and elementary. Actually, they are not simple at all, but they *have* simplified and improved our lives.

Go On ▶

Student Name _____

Now answer Numbers 1 through 9 on your Answer Sheet.
Base your answers on the article "Living Better, Thanks
to Inventions!"

1 Read this sentence from the article.

> **In addition, the automobile helped people interact
> with each other by bringing them closer together.**

Which word means about the SAME as *interact*?

A. relax   C. connect

B. argue   D. disconnect

2 Read this sentence from the article.

> **The wheelchair, for example, assists people who
> cannot walk because of physical problems.**

What is the BEST definition of *wheelchair*?

F. an ambulance

G. a type of furniture

H. a chair with a motor

I. a chair mounted on wheels

3 Read this sentence from the article.

> **A badly broken leg set in an inflexible, rigid plaster
> cast would keep you off your feet for months.**

Which word in the sentence helps to define *rigid*?

A. cast   C. months

B. broken   D. inflexible

© Macmillan/McGraw-Hill

4 Read this sentence from the article.

> **Because these inventions are so familiar to us and we use them every day, they may seem simple and elementary.**

Which word means about the SAME as *elementary*?

- **F.** basic
- **G.** clever
- **H.** school
- **I.** troublesome

5 You can tell that there are glittering generalities in the first paragraph because the author

- **A.** makes broad and vague statements.
- **B.** says that everyone agrees with the statements.
- **C.** quotes a famous person to support the statements.
- **D.** uses many words that may create strong emotions.

6 Which technique of persuasion does the author use in the third paragraph?

- **F.** testimonial
- **G.** bandwagon
- **H.** loaded words
- **I.** glittering generalities

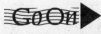

Student Name _____

7 Which technique of persuasion is used in the caption under the second drawing?

    A. testimonial

    B. bandwagon

    C. loaded words

    D. glittering generalities

8 Which two techniques of persuasion does the author use in the fifth paragraph?

    F. bandwagon and testimonial

    G. testimonial and loaded words

    H. glittering generalities and bandwagon

    I. loaded words and glittering generalities

Go On ▶

9 What does the author want readers to think about the importance of inventions? Describe the techniques of persuasion the author uses and whether they are effective. Use information and details from the article to support your answer.

_____

_____

_____

_____

_____

_____

_____

_____

_____

Student Name _____

Read and answer questions 10-12 on your Answer Sheet.

10 Which word is spelled incorrectly?

    A. cycle

    B. salute

    C. echoe

    D. mortal

11 Read this sentence.

> **The first meeting about the <u>Olympics</u> will be held in <u>January</u> on the hotel <u>teracce</u> next to the <u>ocean</u>.**

Which underlined word is spelled incorrectly?

    F. ocean

    G. teracce

    H. January

    I. Olympics

12 Read this sentence.

> **The <u>gracious</u> waiter served the <u>furious</u> child a <u>gigantic</u> bowl of <u>cerael</u>.**

Which underlined word is spelled incorrectly?

    A. cerael

    B. furious

    C. gigantic

    D. gracious

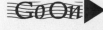

Student Name _____

Read the first part of a story called "Lucy." Choose the word or words that correctly complete questions 13 and 14.

Lucy

Lucy liked to be busy every minute of the day. When she (13) to do, she felt unhappy. Then she would ask everyone in her house, "What can I do for you?"

Lucy's mother liked that her daughter offered to help others. But she thought that Lucy should sometimes be still and simply think—or maybe enjoy nature.

One day Lucy's mother said, "Lucy, why don't you go outside and relax in the backyard this morning?"

"I (14) fun relaxing, Mom," Lucy replied. "There are too many more interesting things to do."

 13 Which answer should go in blank (13)?

   F. didn't have nothing

   G. didn't have anything

   H. didn't have not a thing

14 Which answer should go in blank (14)?

   A. don't ever have any

   B. don't never have no

   C. don't never have any

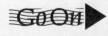

Student Name _____

Read and answer question 15 on your Answer Sheet.

15 Which sentence below does NOT contain a **negative**?

　　F. I have nothing to bring to the party.

　　G. I never said anything about the mistake.

　　H. I need to think of something interesting to do.

STOP

Student Name _____

Student Evaluation Chart

Tested Skills	Number Correct	Percent Correct
Vocabulary Strategies: *Synonyms*, 1; *context clues*, 2, 3, 4	/4	%
Reading Comprehension: *Techniques of persuasion*, 5, 6, 7, 8	/4	%
Short response: *Techniques of persuasion*, 9	/2	%
Spelling: *Words from mythology*, 10, 11, 12	/3	%
Grammar, Mechanics, and Usage: *Correct double negatives*, 13, 14; *negatives*, 15	/3	%
Total Weekly Test Score	**/16**	**%**

Correlations

Item	FCAT Assessed Benchmarks*	New Sunshine State Standards
1	LA.A.1.2.3	LA.5.1.6.8
2	LA.A.1.2.3	LA.5.1.6.3
3	LA.A.1.2.3	LA.5.1.6.3
4	LA.A.1.2.3	LA.5.1.6.3
5	L.A.A.2.2.3	LA.5.1.7.2
6	L.A.A.2.2.3	LA.5.1.7.2
7	L.A.A.2.2.3	LA.5.1.7.2
8	L.A.A.2.2.3	LA.5.1.7.2
9	L.A.A.2.2.3	LA.5.1.7.2
10		LA.5.3.4.1
11		LA.5.3.4.1
12		LA.5.3.4.1
13		LA.5.3.4.4
14		LA.5.3.4.4
15		LA.5.3.4.4

* See benchmarks and standards on pages 379–384.

Name _____

Date _____

FCAT Format Weekly Assessment

TESTED SKILLS AND STRATEGIES

- **Vocabulary Strategies**
- **Reading Comprehension**
- **Spelling**
- **Grammar, Mechanics, and Usage**

**Macmillan
McGraw-Hill**

Read the article "Up, Up, and Away!" before answering
Numbers 1 through 9.

Up, Up, and Away!

More than a century before the Wright brothers' famous plane flight, a different type of object rose into the sky. It was a balloon filled with heated air.

The date was June 4, 1783, and the place was France. Two brothers named Montgolfier launched the very first hot-air balloon. It was made of four huge pieces of fabric and paper, held together by almost 2,000 buttons. The balloon stayed in the air about ten minutes. There were no passengers because that would have been too dangerous.

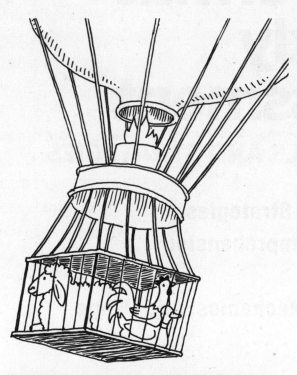

Before humans flew in one of their hot-air balloons, the Montgolfiers sent up a sheep, a duck, and a rooster. The eight-minute flight was launched from the grounds of the French king's palace.

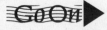

© Macmillan/McGraw–Hill

After this historic event, interest in balloons grew quickly. Inventors began competing to see who would make the safest balloon and take the longest flight. Some people continued to work on balloons filled with heated air. Others developed balloons filled with hydrogen gas, which is lighter than air.

A few months after the flight of the Montgolfier balloon, another first in balloon history took place. A Frenchman named Jacques Charles launched a beautiful balloon made of silk. It was filled with hydrogen gas.

In November of that same year, the Montgolfier brothers again made history. A giant balloon they had constructed carried humans into the air for the first time. One of the passengers was a French science teacher who had helped with the Montgolfier flight of the animals. His companion was a French nobleman. The two men sailed over Paris for 25 minutes. The hot air produced by a fire of burning straw was used to inflate the giant balloon. The balloon caught on fire, but no one was hurt.

In 1785, a Frenchman and an American crossed the English Channel in a hydrogen gas balloon. It was a very dangerous flight. The men barely escaped plunging into the ocean. They made it across the channel by abandoning most of their supplies.

The first balloon flight in the United States traveled from Philadelphia, Pennsylvania, to New Jersey in 1793. George Washington was one of the spectators. He watched as the anchored balloon was released so that it could soar into the air. Balloons had officially entered into United States history.

© Macmillan/McGraw–Hill

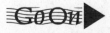

The first flight across the English Channel was very risky.

The first hot-air and hydrogen balloons were used by adventurers. But some people soon realized that they also could be used for military purposes, such as delivering messages across long distances. During World War II, they also served another purpose. Wires were strung between balloons, forming a dense trap that military planners hoped would stop an enemy bomber.

Today meteorological balloons carry scientific tools, such as barometers, that measure the air pressure, wind speed, and ozone levels. So, while hot-air balloons often are used for recreation, they still are used for serious purposes as well.

Now answer Numbers 1 through 9 on your Answer Sheet.
Base your answers on the article "Up, Up, and Away!"

1 Read this sentence from the article.

> **Others developed balloons filled with hydrogen gas, which is lighter than air.**

What is the Greek root of the word *hydrogen*?

A. hyg   **C.** ogen

B. drog   **D.** hydro

2 Read this sentence from the article.

> **The hot air produced by a fire of burning straw was used to inflate the giant balloon.**

What does *inflate* mean?

F. catch on fire

G. reduce in size

H. fill with gas or air

I. increase in weight

3 Read this sentence from the article.

> **He watched as the anchored balloon was released so that it could soar into the air.**

What does *anchored* mean?

A. secured

B. released

C. launched

D. equipped

Go On ▶

Read this sentence from the article.

Wires were strung between balloons, forming a dense trap that military planners hoped would stop an enemy bomber.

Which word in the sentence helps you to understand the meaning of the word *dense*?

F. trap

G. enemy

H. military

I. balloons

5 The Greek root *baro* means "pressure." Which word below has *baro* as a root?

A. baron

B. barracks

C. baroness

D. barometer

6 The caption under the first illustration includes a detail that BEST supports the idea that

F. early balloon flight was experimental.

G. from the beginning, balloon flight could serve several purposes.

H. members of French royalty were involved in early balloon flight.

I. fierce competition among inventors occurred during early balloon flight.

© Macmillan/McGraw-Hill

7 Based on the article, which statement applies to BOTH types of balloons?

    A. They were beautiful.

    B. They were dangerous.

    C. They were filled with heated air.

    D. They were constructed of paper.

8 Which detail from the article is MOST relevant to the development of early balloons?

    F. Balloons were used in wars to deliver messages.

    G. The first balloon that carried humans caught on fire during the flight.

    H. Inventors began to compete to see who could make a successful balloon.

    I. George Washington witnessed the first balloon flight in the United States.

GO ON

9 What information in the article "Up, Up, and Away!" supports the generalization that balloons fueled by hot air or hydrogen gas have many uses? Use details from the article to support your answer.

_____

_____

_____

_____

_____

_____

_____

_____

_____

_____

_____

_____

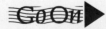

Student Name _____

Read and answer questions 10–12 on your Answer Sheet.

10 Which word is spelled incorrectly?

    A. tripod

    B. century

    C. universe

    D. byweekly

11 Read this sentence.

> **The <u>unicorn</u> and the <u>centepede</u> sang their song in <u>unison</u>, and the dog made it a <u>trio</u>.**

Which underlined word is spelled incorrectly?

    F. trio

    G. unison

    H. unicorn

    I. centepede

12 Read this sentence.

> **The bike store near the <u>unaversity</u> had a <u>tricycle</u>, a <u>unicycle</u>, and a <u>bicycle</u> for sale.**

Which underlined word is spelled incorrectly?

    A. bicycle

    B. tricycle

    C. unicycle

    D. unaversity

Read and answer questions 13–15 on your Answer Sheet.

13 Which sentence below contains a **prepositional phrase**?

    F. The squirrels chased each other.

    G. The birds flew by over our heads.

    H. The students sat still all afternoon.

14 In which sentence below is all **punctuation** correct?

    A. By the end of next week, we should be the district champions.

    B. During the football game we cheered, loudly for our favorite player.

    C. Between the two, football teams, there is a serious sense of competition.

15 Which sentence below contains a **preposition**?

    F. The spinner went round and round.

    G. Many students like the new teacher.

    H. Samantha sat beside her grandmother.

STOP

Student Name _____

Grade 5 • Unit 6 • Week 4
Student Evaluation Chart

Tested Skills	Number Correct	Percent Correct
Vocabulary Strategies: *Greek roots, 1, 5; context clues, 2, 3, 4*	/5	%
Reading Comprehension: *Relevant facts and details, 6, 7, 8*	/3	%
Extended response: *Relevant facts and details, 9*	/4	%
Spelling: *Number prefixes* uni-, bi-, tri-, cent-, *10, 11, 12*	/3	%
Grammar, Mechanics, and Usage: *Prepositions and prepositional phrases, 13, 15; using commas to separate prepositional phrases introducing sentences, 14*	/3	%

Total Weekly Test Score	/18	%

Correlations

Item	FCAT Assessed Benchmarks*	New Sunshine State Standards
1		LA.5.1.6.11
2	LA.A.1.2.3	LA.5.1.6.3
3	LA.A.1.2.3	LA.5.1.6.3
4	LA.A.1.2.3	LA.5.1.6.3
5		LA.5.1.6.11
6	LA.A.2.2.1	LA.5.2.2.2
7	LA.A.2.2.1	LA.5.2.2.2
8	LA.A.2.2.1	LA.5.2.2.2
9	LA.A.2.2.1	LA.5.2.2.2
10		LA.5.3.4.1
11		LA.5.3.4.1
12		LA.5.3.4.1
13		LA.5.3.4.4
14		LA.5.3.4.3
15		LA.5.3.4.4

* See benchmarks and standards on pages 379–384.

Name _____

Date _____

FCAT Format Weekly Assessment

TESTED SKILLS AND STRATEGIES

- **Vocabulary Strategies**
- **Reading Comprehension**
- **Spelling**
- **Grammar, Mechanics, and Usage**

Read the story "All in a Day's Work" before answering Numbers 1 through 9.

All in a Day's Work

Dr. Schwartz studied the elements of soil and plant life. Because of her work, she spent a great deal of time looking for specimens. She searched the woods, looking under rocks, on leaves, and in the soil for interesting plants to use in her experiments.

One day she found some algae in a dirty, murky pond. She carefully placed the algae in a plastic bag. Then she picked some lichens off a tree. Finally, before ending her search for that day, she scooped some soil from the ground. The soil contained bacteria that she needed to complete her research.

Back in her biology lab, Dr. Schwartz first performed tests on the soil she had collected. She was just about to start her experiments on the algae when a fellow scientist, Dr. Rao, threw open the door to her lab and announced, "We need you to look at our latest experiment. Please come to my lab."

"I don't think I can get away right now," Dr. Schwartz said.

"Just for a few moments," he pleaded. "Something unusual has occurred."

Dr. Schwartz wiped the dirt off her hands and followed Dr. Rao down the hall. "This had better be good," she told him.

Go On ▶

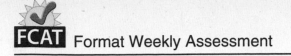
"We had a dormant mixture," Dr. Rao explained as they walked quickly. "It was inactive, but—" He paused as he opened the door.

"Not any more!" Dr. Schwartz yelled. The mixture had erupted all over the lab! Thick slime was shooting out of beakers, like a volcano exploding all over. The slime hung from the ceiling and covered the floor.

"I'm just an observer," Dr. Schwartz said, trying to stay calm. "I'm not conducting this experiment. But this does look dangerous. We'd better get out of here!"

Dr. Schwartz, Dr. Rao, and the other scientists who had been working in his lab backed out of the room and slammed the door behind them.

Go On ▶

Dr. Schwartz said, "We have to do something before it slimes the entire building. Let me handle this." She ran to her lab and, in a matter of seconds, was back. Then she flung open the door to Dr. Rao's lab and threw in a bag of dirt.

She smiled as she observed the slime being scoured away. Dr. Rao and the other scientists watched in disbelief. Dr. Schwartz explained, "The compounds in the soil I'm studying have anti-slime components. I discovered the soil in an area that was devoid of algae—not a single one was to be found. But I never expected that my discovery would come in handy so soon." Then she turned to leave and said, "Well, back to work for me."

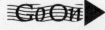

**Now answer Numbers 1 through 9 on your Answer Sheet.
Base your answers on the story "All in a Day's Work."**

1 Read this sentence from the story.

> **One day she found some algae in a dirty,
> murky pond.**

Which word means almost the SAME as *murky*?

A. dark

B. clear

C. deep

D. large

2 Read this sentence from the story.

> **Back in her biology lab, Dr. Schwartz first performed
> tests on the soil she had collected.**

Which word below does NOT have the same Greek root
as *biology*?

F. bionic   H. biologist

G. biplane   I. biosphere

3 Read these sentences from the story.

> **"We had a dormant mixture," Dr. Rao explained as
> they walked quickly. "It was inactive, but—"**

The Greek root *dorm* means "sleep." Which word below has
the SAME root as *dormant*?

A. dorsal   C. dormitory

B. doormat   D. doorknob

Go On

4 Read this sentence from the story.

The mixture had erupted all over the lab!

Which word means about the SAME as *erupted*?

F. melted

G. softened

H. exploded

I. dissolved

5 What does Dr. Schwartz do FIRST?

A. She finds algae in a dirty pond.

B. She goes to Dr. Rao's lab at his request.

C. She carefully scoops dirt from the ground.

D. She performs tests on items she has collected.

6 What happens AFTER Dr. Schwartz sees the slime erupting?

F. She searches the woods.

G. She performs test on soil.

H. She places pond algae in a bag.

I. She runs to her lab to get something.

7 Which event happens LAST in the story?

    A. Dr. Schwartz throws dirt on a lab floor.

    B. Dr. Rao shows Dr. Schwartz slime in his lab.

    C. Dr. Rao watches something amazing happen.

    D. Dr. Schwartz discovers soil that contains no algae.

8 Read the sentences in the box.

> **1. Dr. Schwartz goes to Dr. Rao's lab.**
>
> **2. Dr. Rao goes to see Dr. Schwartz.**
>
> **3. Dr. Schwartz leaves Dr. Rao's lab to return to work.**
>
> **4. Dr. Rao and Dr. Schwartz watch slime erupt.**

In what order do these events take place in the story?

    F. 2, 1, 4, 3

    G. 3, 1, 2, 4

    H. 2, 1, 3, 4

    I. 1, 2, 4, 3

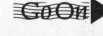

9 What would have happened if Dr. Schwartz had found the slime-fighting soil at the END of the story instead of at the BEGINNING? Use details and information from the story to support your answer.

READ
THINK
EXPLAIN

_____

_____

_____

_____

_____

_____

_____

_____

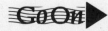

Student Name _____

Read and answer questions 10–12 on your Answer Sheet.

10 Which word is spelled incorrectly?

   A. likable

   B. possible

   C. laughible

   D. unbelievable

11 Read this sentence.

> The <u>convertable</u> car had a <u>collapsible</u> roof, which made the car <u>enjoyable</u> and <u>comfortable</u> in the mild spring weather.

Which underlined word is spelled incorrectly?

   F. enjoyable

   G. collapsible

   H. convertable

   I. comfortable

12 Read this sentence.

> The store sold many items, including <u>sensible</u> shoes, <u>suitible</u> clothing, <u>affordable</u> gifts, and glasses that were not <u>breakable</u>.

Which underlined word is spelled incorrectly?

   A. suitible

   B. sensible

   C. breakable

   D. affordable

Student Name _____

Read and answer questions 13–15 on your Answer Sheet.

13 In which sentence below is all **punctuation** correct?

   F. Before we drove off we, locked the car doors!

   G. Before we drove off, we locked the car doors.

   H. Before, we drove off, we locked the car doors.

14 Read the sentences in the box.

> **I saw many fish and shells.**
>
> **They were colorful.**

Which sentence below BEST combines the sentences in the box?

   A. I saw many colorful fish and shells.

   B. I saw many fish and shells that were colorful.

   C. I saw many fish and shells, and they were colorful.

15 Read the sentences in the box.

> **We were outside.**
>
> **The cat knocked over a bowl while we were out there.**
>
> **The bowl was my mom's favorite.**

Which sentence below correctly combines the sentences in the box?

F. While outside, the cat knocked over my mom's favorite bowl.

G. The cat knocked over my mom's favorite bowl while we were outside.

H. We were outside and the cat knocked over a bowl and it was my mom's favorite.

STOP

Grade 5 • Unit 6 • Week 5
Student Evaluation Chart

Tested Skills	Number Correct	Percent Correct
Vocabulary Strategies: *Context clues, 1, 4; Greek roots, 2, 3*	/4	%
Reading Comprehension: *Chronological order, 5, 6, 7, 8*	/4	%
Short response: *Chronological order, 9*	/2	%
Spelling: *Words with* -able, -ible, *10, 11, 12*	/3	%
Grammar, Mechanics, and Usage: *Review of punctuation marks, 13; sentence combining, 14, 15*	/3	%
Total Weekly Test Score	/16	%

Correlations

Item	FCAT Assessed Benchmarks*	New Sunshine State Standards
1	LA.A.1.2.3	LA.5.1.6.3
2		LA.5.1.6.11
3		LA.5.1.6.11
4	LA.A.1.2.3	LA.5.1.7.5
5	LA.A.2.2.7	LA.5.1.7.5
6	LA.A.2.2.7	LA.5.1.7.5
7	LA.A.2.2.7	LA.5.1.7.5
8	LA.A.2.2.7	LA.5.1.7.5
9	LA.A.2.2.7	LA.5.1.7.5
10		LA.5.3.4.1
11		LA.5.3.4.1
12		LA.5.3.4.1
13		LA.5.3.4.3
14		LA.5.3.2.2
15		LA.5.3.2.2

* See benchmarks and standards on pages 379–384.

Answer Keys

Unit 1

Week 1

1. D
2. I
3. D
4. H
5. B
6. H
7. D
8. I

9. **Top-Score Response:**

In the fourth paragraph, Aisha is thinking of a conversation with José that she had a year before. The story makes it seem as if she is really back at that time. She has to shake herself to bring herself back to the present time.

10. D
11. F
12. A
13. G
14. A
15. G

Week 2

1. D
2. G
3. A
4. I
5. B
6. I
7. D
8. I

9. **Top-Score Response:**

The golf course is 30 miles wide. The sand pit is like a desert, and the water hazard is actually a lake. This golf course is too big to be real, just like Paul Bunyan.

10. A
11. I
12. A
13. H
14. D
15. H

Week 3

1. D
2. F
3. D
4. G
5. D
6. G
7. A
8. I

9. **Top-Score Response:**

Animals in hot deserts hunt during the cool nights, while animals in cold deserts hunt during the warmer daylight hours. Both sets of animals hunt during the part of the day when the temperature is the most comfortable.

10. D
11. G
12. A
13. H
14. C
15. G

Week 4

1. C
2. I
3. A
4. F
5. A
6. I
7. D
8. F

9. **Top-Score Response:**

To help readers understand how satellites help scientists and are their "eyes in the sky," the author describes different kinds of satellites. Some are used to explore Earth and other planets and some carry TV, radio, and phone signals over long distances. Other satellites locate objects like ships, planes, and cars, or send weather information to computers on Earth.

10. A
11. G
12. D
13. F
14. C
15. G

© Macmillan/McGraw-Hill

Week 5

1. C
2. I
3. C
4. I
5. D
6. F
7. B
8. F

9. **Top-Score Response:**

Ellen and Ben will take the weather conditions more seriously before going on another ski trip. They also probably will plan to ski only in areas they know are watched over by ski patrol staff and their rescue dogs.

10. B
11. H
12. D
13. G
14. C
15. H

Unit 2

Week 1

1. D
2. F
3. D
4. G
5. A
6. H
7. C
8. H

9. **Top-Score Response:**

Kyle and Mr. Jackson already have a strong friendship when the story begins. Kyle looks up to and trusts Mr. Jackson. One way Mr. Jackson influences Kyle is by helping him realize that people should help and look out for each other. Kyle learns to be a more thoughtful, considerate person.

10. C
11. G
12. B
13. H
14. A
15. G

Week 2

1. C
2. H
3. C
4. F
5. C
6. F
7. D
8. F

9. **Top-Score Response:**

The main idea of the article "Super Snakes" is that snakes are misunderstood. They would not cause so much fear as they do if people knew more about them.

Snakes have many interesting features. For example, they can hide from predators because of the patterns and coloring on their skin, which help them to blend in with their environment. Also, their tongues are part of their sense of smell.

Knowing more about snakes can make people less afraid of them. It still is important to be careful around snakes, but they really are very interesting creatures!

10. B
11. H
12. D
13. G
14. B
15. F

Week 3

1. B
2. F
3. D
4. G
5. C
6. F
7. A
8. G

9. **Top-Score Response:**

To help readers understand life in the Middle Ages, the author mentions details about the social system, such as who belonged to different social classes and the fact that kings and queens owned the most land and had the most power. The author also provides details about the education system. For example, most children did not get any education. Some children learned a trade or craft, but only a few wealthy children got an education in schools.

10. C
11. H
12. A
13. F
14. B
15. H

Week 4

1. B
2. G
3. C
4. F
5. D
6. I
7. A
8. H

9. **Top-Score Response:**

Marisol does two things to try to solve her problem. First, she tries to make her own costume. When that does not work, she helps Mrs. Blanco so the seamstress will have the time to make her costume. These efforts reveal that Marisol is a creative problem solver.

10. C
11. G
12. D
13. G
14. B
15. F

Week 5

1. C
2. G
3. D
4. F
5. C
6. F
7. B
8. H

9. **Top-Score Response:**

Cowboys and cowgirls who work on ranches must not mind hard and possibly dangerous work. They need to have certain traditional skills, like horse riding, but they also have to be willing to develop different skills as ranch life changes. Modern cowboys and cowgirls have to know how to adapt to change.

10. A
11. I
12. C
13. F
14. C
15. I

Unit 3

Week 1

1. D
2. H
3. C
4. H
5. A
6. I
7. D
8. F

9. **Top-Score Response:**

    The story states that both the Patriots and his father praised William for his work. Also, many years later, William loved to tell his grandchildren stories about his spy missions during Revolutionary War. These details show that he was very proud of his role in the war.

10. C
11. I
12. C
13. G
14. B
15. G

Week 2

1. C
2. G
3. A
4. F
5. B
6. F
7. A
8. F

9. **Top-Score Response:**

    This statement is a fact. The article gives many examples to support it.

    Women's struggle to win the right to vote began in 1848. For the next several decades women made few gains, despite a continued struggle. Starting in 1869, women in some states and territories were able to take part in elections. But the U.S. Congress did not pass an amendment that gave all American women the right to vote until 1919, and it was not ratified until 1920.

10. A
11. G
12. B
13. G
14. A
15. F

Week 3

1. B
2. H
3. D
4. H
5. C
6. F
7. B
8. I

9. **Top-Score Response:**

    The author is trying to persuade readers to help the environment. To accomplish this, the author tells them they can help the environment by using as few of the earth's natural resources as possible. Then the author explains simple ways to reduce the use of those resources.

10. D
11. G
12. D
13. H
14. A
15. F

Week 4

1. B
2. G
3. D
4. F
5. C
6. F
7. A
8. I

9. **Top-Score Response:**

    Matthew changes a lot during the story "Life with Trees." In the beginning of the story, Matthew is cold-hearted. He commits crimes against nature. He lets his factories pollute rivers and has trees cut down for money. By the end of the story, however, he has grown to love nature. He helps to preserve nature and later decides to share his estate with others.

10. C
11. G
12. B
13. H
14. C
15. G

Week 5

1. D
2. I
3. B
4. H
5. A
6. H
7. A
8. F

9. **Top-Score Response:**

Rasheed is good-natured, but he does not handle pressure well, and he is not persistent. When he does not do well at the video game, he wants to do something different the following weekend.

10. C
11. F
12. C
13. G
14. B
15. F

Unit 4

Week 1

1. A
2. F
3. C
4. G
5. A
6. I
7. D
8. I

9. **Top-Score Response:**

The protesters do not want social change and are against the integration of the school. They react in anger to the students, even though judges made the decision that led to the students attending that school.

10. B
11. G
12. C
13. F
14. B
15. H

Week 2

1. D
2. G
3. C
4. H
5. C
6. I
7. C
8. H

9. **Top-Score Response:**

By using the word "good" in the title to describe a method of defense, the author lets the reader know that he thinks that both the jackrabbit's and Vicente's actions were smart and correct. The last sentence of the story also supports this idea.

10. A
11. F
12. A
13. F
14. C
15. H

Week 3

1. B
2. G
3. D
4. I
5. D
6. G
7. C
8. I

9. **Top-Score Response:**

Democracy gives the citizens of a country the power to elect their leaders and representatives. The system of checks and balances in a democracy works well because the three branches of government share power. One branch cannot gain too much power over the other branches. For these reasons, a democracy is the most effective form of government.

10. C
11. F
12. C
13. F
14. A
15. H

Week 4

1. A
2. G
3. C
4. I
5. A
6. I
7. B
8. F

9. **Top-Score Response:**

In the second, third, and fourth paragraphs of "The Life of a Hurricane," the author describes how a hurricane develops, from its beginning to its end. The conditions that must be present for a hurricane even to start forming are discussed first. Then the author describes the conditions that make a hurricane grow. The final point of the description tells how and why a hurricane ends.

10. A
11. H
12. D
13. G
14. B
15. G

Week 5

1. A
2. F
3. C
4. H
5. B
6. I
7. D
8. H

9. **Top-Score Response:**

Fish Hawk leaves because he is tired of Raven's lies. The author shows that Raven's lies succeed for a while. However, in the end Raven is left without food and without his friend Fish Hawk.

10. A
11. G
12. D
13. G
14. A
15. H

Unit 5

Week 1

1. D
2. H
3. A
4. H
5. A
6. I
7. D
8. H

9. **Top-Score Response:**

The trip to the South Pole from the base camp was going to be long and would take place in harsh weather. Amundsen and his team set up depots filled with supplies before starting the trip. They could go to the depots for shelter and to get supplies on their way to the South Pole.

10. D
11. H
12. A
13. F
14. B
15. G

Week 2

1. D
2. I
3. A
4. H
5. C
6. H
7. C
8. G

9. **Top-Score Response:**

The story "A Matter of Taste" leaves the reader with an important message about life. This message is that it is good to try new things instead of always being satisfied with what you are familiar with. Tasting foods from other cultures is one way to try something new. By doing this you can learn about different cultures. This is what Claudia realizes after she has the dream about visiting other countries and seeing the delicious-looking foods the people are eating.

10. D
11. G
12. D
13. F
14. B
15. G

Week 3

1. A
2. H
3. A
4. I
5. D
6. H
7. A
8. I

9. **Top-Score Response:**

Birds and cattle often eat together. When birds sense danger, they make lots of noise and fly away. This warns the cattle, which then leave the area.

10. C
11. I
12. C
13. G
14. B
15. F

Week 4

1. B
2. F
3. D
4. I
5. B
6. G
7. A
8. F

9. **Top-Score Response:**

The author most likely believes that the Navajo Code Talkers were smart and brave and that they were responsible for saving many lives. I think this because the author has the speaker say that the Code Talkers were a crucial part of every battle that took place in the Pacific Corridor for three years. The speaker also says that these men helped assure victory in the war.

10. D
11. F
12. A
13. H
14. B
15. F

Week 5

1. D
2. I
3. A
4. F
5. D
6. H
7. C
8. H

9. **Top-Score Response:**

The setting, a whale-watching tour boat in the ocean on a warm winter day, is important to the story's plot for two reasons. First, while Anita and Zach are watching whales from the boat she becomes interested as he tells her about what an oceanographer does. Second, Anita likes the idea that this beautiful setting is where an oceanographer would work.

10. A
11. H
12. D
13. H
14. C
15. F

Unit 6

Week 1

1. B
2. G
3. D
4. I
5. B
6. G
7. D
8. H

9. **Top-Score Response:**

After Hans trades the goose for the grinding stone, he loses it when it falls into a stream. Once it is gone, he realizes how good it feels not to have the stone or anything else in his possession. Everything he has owned has caused him a problem. By contrast, now that he owns nothing he feels free.

10. A
11. G
12. B
13. F
14. C
15. F

Week 2

1. B
2. F
3. A
4. G
5. D
6. F
7. B
8. G

9. **Top-Score Response:**

Randall has a hard time camping. He is easily frustrated. His complaining and yelling about the problems he is having with the tent are a good example of this. He gets more and more upset. He does not realize that things would be easier if he calmed down.

Randall needs to learn to be more patient and to appreciate his surroundings. Nick realizes this and tells Randall to relax and enjoy the scenery.

10. B
11. I
12. C
13. H
14. D
15. H

Week 3

1. C
2. I
3. D
4. F
5. A
6. H
7. D
8. G

9. **Top-Score Response:**

The author wants readers to believe that inventions have improved lives and that without them we would not be happy. To persuade readers, the author uses loaded words such as *mayhem* and *indispensable*. There also are glittering generalities in the first paragraph. Also, the author includes a testimonial.

10. C
11. G
12. A
13. G
14. A
15. H

Week 4

1. D
2. H
3. A
4. F
5. D
6. F
7. B
8. H

9. **Top-Score Response:**

Over the years, hot-air and hydrogen gas balloons have had many uses. They are used for pleasure. The author says they were used by "adventurers" and today they are used for "recreation." They have been used for military purposes, to deliver messages and to form a dense trap that would stop enemy bombers. Finally, they have been used for scientific purposes. The author says they carry scientific tools such as barometers to measure weather conditions.

10. D
11. I
12. D
13. G
14. A
15. H

Week 5

1. A
2. G
3. C
4. H
5. A
6. I
7. C
8. F

9. **Top-Score Response:**

Because Dr. Schwartz finds the soil and tests it at the beginning of the story, she can solve Dr. Rao's problem with the erupting slime. If she had found the soil at the end, the story and the outcome would have been very different. She could not have solved the slime problem.

10. C
11. H
12. A
13. G
14. A
15. G

Constructed-Response Rubrics

Use the rubrics below to score the short and extended responses in the Reading tests.

Rubric for Short-Response Questions	
Score	**Description**
2	The student's response demonstrates a thorough understanding of the comprehension skills needed to answer the question. Details and examples are used to support the answer and clearly come from the text.
1	The student's response demonstrates a partial understanding of the comprehension skills needed to answer the question. Some of the support and important details and/or examples are too general or are left out.
0	The student's response demonstrates a complete lack of understanding of the question or the student has left the answer blank.

Rubric for Extended-Response Questions	
Score	**Description**
4	The student's response demonstrates a thorough understanding of the comprehension skills needed to answer the question. Details and examples are used to support the answer and clearly come from the text.
3	The student's response demonstrates an understanding of the comprehension skills needed to answer the question. Details and examples used as support are not complete or are not text-based.
2	The student's response demonstrates a partial understanding of the comprehension skills needed to answer the question. Some of the support and important details and/or examples are too general or are left out.
1	The student's response is incomplete and does not demonstrate an understanding of the question.
0	The student's response demonstrates a complete lack of understanding of the question or the student has left the answer blank.

FCAT Reading Assessed Benchmarks Grades 3-5	Grade 5 Sunshine State Standards
LA.A.1.2.3 Uses simple strategies to determine meaning and increase vocabulary for reading, including the use of prefixes, suffixes, root words, multiple meanings, antonyms, synonyms, and word relationships.	**LA.5.1.6.3** use context clues to determine meanings of unfamiliar words **LA.5.1.6.7** use meaning of familiar base words and affixes to determine meanings of unfamiliar complex words **LA.5.1.6.8** use knowledge of antonyms, synonyms, homophones, and homographs to determine meanings of words **LA.5.1.6.9** determine the correct meaning of words with multiple meanings in context
LA.A.2.2.1 Reads text and determines the main idea or essential message, identifies relevant supporting details and facts, and arranges events in chronological order.	**LA.5.1.7.3** determine the main idea or essential message in grade-level text through inferring, paraphrasing, summarizing, and identifying relevant details [**LA.5.2.2.2** use information form the text to answer questions related to explicitly stated main ideas or relevant details]
LA.A.2.2.2 Identifies the author's purpose in a simple text. (Includes LA.A.2.2.3 Recognizes when a text is primarily intended to persuade.)	**LA.5.1.7.2** identify the author's purpose (e.g., to persuade, inform, entertain, explain) and how an author's perspective influences text
LA.A.2.2.7 Recognizes the use of comparison and contrast in a text.	**L.A.5.1.7.5** identify the text structure an author uses (e.g., comparison/contrast, cause/effect, and sequence of events) and explain how it impacts meaning in text
LA.A.2.2.8 Selects and uses a variety of appropriate reference materials, including multiple representations of information such as maps, charts, and photos, to gather information for research projects. (Includes LA.A.2.2.5 Reads and organizes information for a variety of purposes, including making a report, conducting interviews, taking a test, and performing an authentic task.)	**LA.5.1.7.1** explain the purpose of text features (e.g., format, graphics, diagrams, illustrations, charts, and maps), use prior knowledge to make and confirm predictions, and establish a purpose for reading [**LA.5.2.2.1** locate, explain, and use information from text features (e.g., tables of contents, glossary, index, transition words/phrases, headings, subheadings, charts, graphs, illustrations)]
LA.E.1.2.2 Understands the development of plot and how conflicts are resolved in a story.	**LA.5.2.1.2** locate and analyze the elements of plot structure, including exposition, setting, character development, rising/falling action, problem/resolution, and theme in a variety of fiction
LA.E.1.2.3 Knows the similarities and differences among the characters, settings, and events presented in various texts.	**LA.5.1.7.7** compare and contrast elements in multiple texts (e.g., settings, characters, problems)
LA.E.2.2.1 Recognizes cause-and-effect relationships in literary texts. [Applies to fiction, nonfiction, poetry, and drama.]	**LA.5.1.7.4** identify cause-and-effect relationships in text

New Sunshine State Standards
Grade 5 Reading and Language Arts

Grade 5: Reading Process

Phonics/Word Analysis

Standard: The student demonstrates knowledge of the alphabetic principle and applies grade level phonics skills to read text.

The student will:

LA.5.1.4.1 understand spelling patterns;

LA.5.1.4.2 recognize structural analysis; and

LA.5.1.4.3 use language structure to read multi-syllabic words in text.

Fluency

Standard: The student demonstrates the ability to read grade level text orally with accuracy, appropriate rate, and expression.

The student will:

LA.5.1.5.1 demonstrate the ability to read grade level text; and

LA.5.1.5.2 adjust reading rate based on purpose, text difficulty, form, and style.

Vocabulary Development

Standard: The student uses multiple strategies to develop grade appropriate vocabulary.

The student will:

LA.5.1.6.1 use new vocabulary that is introduced and taught directly;

LA.5.1.6.2 listen to, read, and discuss familiar and conceptually challenging text;

LA.5.1.6.3 use context clues to determine meanings of unfamiliar words;

LA.5.1.6.4 categorize key vocabulary and identify salient features;

LA.5.1.6.5 relate new vocabulary to familiar words;

LA.5.1.6.6 identify "shades of meaning" in related words (e.g., blaring, loud);

LA.5.1.6.7 use meaning of familiar base words and affixes to determine meanings of unfamiliar complex words;

LA.5.1.6.8 use knowledge of antonyms, synonyms, homophones, and homographs to determine meanings of words;

LA.5.1.6.9 determine the correct meaning of words with multiple meanings in context;

LA.5.1.6.10 determine meanings of words, pronunciation, parts of speech, etymologies, and alternate word choices by using a dictionary, thesaurus, and digital tools; and

LA.5.1.6.11 use meaning of familiar roots and affixes derived from Greek and Latin to determine meanings of unfamiliar complex words.

Reading Comprehension

Standard: The student uses a variety of strategies to comprehend grade level text.

The student will:

LA.5.1.7.1 explain the purpose of text features (e.g., format, graphics, diagrams, illustrations, charts, and maps), use prior knowledge to make and confirm predictions, and establish a purpose for reading;

LA.5.1.7.2 identify the author's purpose (e.g., to persuade, inform, entertain, explain) and how an author's perspective influences text;

LA.5.1.7.3 determine the main idea or essential message in grade-level text through inferring, paraphrasing, summarizing, and identifying relevant details;

LA.5.1.7.4 identify cause-and-effect relationships in text;

LA.5.1.7.5 identify the text structure an author uses (e.g., comparison/contrast, cause/effect, sequence of events) and explain how it impacts meaning in text;

LA.5.1.7.6 identify themes or topics across a variety of fiction and non-fiction selections;

LA.5.1.7.7 compare and contrast elements in multiple texts (e.g., setting, characters, problems); and

LA.5.1.7.8 use strategies to repair comprehension of grade-appropriate text when self-monitoring indicates confusion, including but not limited to rereading, checking context clues, predicting, note-making, summarizing, using graphic and semantic organizers, questioning, and clarifying by checking other sources.

Grade 5: Literary Analysis

Fiction

Standard: The student identifies, analyzes, and applies knowledge of the elements of a variety of fiction and literary texts to develop a thoughtful response to a literary selection.

The student will:

LA.5.2.1.1 demonstrate knowledge of the characteristics of various genres (e.g., poetry, fiction, short story, dramatic literature) as forms with distinct characteristics and purposes;

LA.5.2.1.2 locate and analyze the elements of plot structure, including exposition, setting, character development, rising/falling action, problem/resolution, and theme in a variety of fiction;

LA.5.2.1.3 demonstrate how rhythm and repetition as well as descriptive and figurative language help to communicate meaning in a poem;

LA.5.2.1.4 identify an author's theme, and use details from the text to explain how the author developed that theme;

LA.5.2.1.5 demonstrate an understanding of a literary selection, and depending on the selection, include evidence from the text, personal experience, and comparison to other text/media;

LA.5.2.1.6 write a book report, review, or critique that identifies the main idea, character(s), setting, sequence of events, conflict, crisis, and resolution;

LA.5.2.1.7 identify and explain an author's use of descriptive, idiomatic, and figurative language (e.g., personification, similes, metaphors, symbolism), and examine how it is used to describe people, feelings, and objects;

LA.5.2.1.8 explain changes in the vocabulary and language patterns of literary texts written across historical periods; and

LA.5.2.1.9 use interest and recommendations of other to select a balance of age- and ability-appropriate fiction materials to read (e.g., novels, historical fiction, mythology, poetry) to expand the core foundation of knowledge necessary to function as a fully literate member of a shared culture.

Non-Fiction

Standard: The student identifies, analyzes, and applies knowledge of the elements of a variety of non-fiction, informational, and expository texts to demonstrate an understanding of the information presented.

The student will:

LA.5.2.2.1 locate, explain, and use information from text features (e.g., table of contents, glossary, index, transition words/phrases, headings, subheadings, charts, graphs, illustrations);

LA.5.2.2.2 use information from the text to answer questions related to explicitly stated main ideas or relevant details;

LA.5.2.2.3 organize information to show understanding (i.e., representing main ideas within text through charting, mapping, paraphrasing, or summarizing);

LA.5.2.2.4 identify the characteristics of a variety of types of text (e.g., reference, newspapers, practical/functional texts); and

LA.5.2.2.5 use interest and recommendations of others to select a balance of age and ability appropriate non-fiction materials to read (e.g., biographies and topical areas, such as animals, science, history) to continue building a core foundation of knowledge.

Grade 5: Writing Process

Pre-Writing

Standard: The student will use prewriting strategies to generate ideas and formulate a plan.

The student will prewrite by:

LA.5.3.1.1 generating ideas from multiple sources (e.g., text, brainstorming, graphic organizer, drawing, writer's notebook, group discussion, printed material) based upon teacher-directed topics and personal interests;

LA.5.3.1.2 determining the purpose (e.g., to entertain, to inform, to communicate, to persuade) and intended audience of a writing piece; and

LA.5.3.1.3 organizing ideas using strategies and tools (e.g., technology, graphic organizer, KWL chart, log) to make a plan for writing that prioritizes ideas and addresses main idea, logical sequence, and the time needed to complete the task.

Drafting

Standard: The student will write a draft appropriate to the topic, audience, and purpose.

The student will draft writing by:

LA.5.3.2.1 using a pre-writing plan to focus on the main idea with ample development of supporting details, elaborating on organized information using descriptive language, supporting details, and word choices appropriate to the selected tone and mood;

LA.5.3.2.2 organizing information into a logical sequence and combining or deleting sentences to enhance clarity; and

LA.5.3.2.3 creating interesting leads by studying the leads of professional authors and experimenting with various types of leads (e.g., an astonishing fact, a dramatic scene).

Revising

Standard: The student will revise and refine the draft for clarity and effectiveness.

The student will revise by:

LA.5.3.3.1 evaluating the draft for development of ideas and content, logical organization, voice, point of view, word choice, and sentence variation;

LA.5.3.3.2 creating clarity and logic by deleting extraneous or repetitious information and tightening plot or central idea through the use of sequential organization, appropriate transitional phrases, and introductory phrases and clauses that vary rhythm and sentence structure;

LA.5.3.3.3 creating precision and interest by expressing ideas vividly through varied language techniques (e.g., foreshadowing, imagery, simile, metaphor, sensory language, connotation, denotation) and modifying word choices using resources and reference materials (e.g., dictionary, thesaurus); and

LA.5.3.3.4 applying appropriate tools or strategies to evaluate and refine the draft (e.g., peer review, checklists, rubrics).

Editing for Language Conventions

Standard: The student will edit and correct the draft for standard language conventions.

The student edits writing for grammar and language conventions, including the correct use of:

LA.5.3.4.1 spelling, using spelling rules, orthographic patterns, generalizations, knowledge of root words, prefixes, suffixes, and knowledge of Greek and Latin root words and using a dictionary, thesaurus, or other resources as necessary;

LA.5.3.4.2 capitalization, including literary titles, nationalities, ethnicities, languages, religions, geographic names and places;

LA.5.3.4.3 punctuation, including commas in clauses, hyphens, and in cited sources, including quotations for exact words from sources;

LA.5.3.4.4 the four basic parts of speech (nouns, verbs, adjectives, adverbs), and subjective, objective, and demonstrative pronouns and singular and plural possessives of nouns; and

LA.5.3.4.5 subject/verb and noun/pronoun agreement in simple and compound sentences.

Publishing

Standard: The student will write a final product for the intended audience.

The student will:

LA.5.3.5.1 prepare writing using technology in a format appropriate to audience and purpose (e.g., manuscript, multimedia);

LA.5.3.5.2 use elements of spacing and design to enhance the appearance of the document and add graphics where appropriate; and

LA.5.3.5.3 share the writing with the intended audience.

Grade 5: Writing Applications

Creative

Standard: The student develops and demonstrates creative writing.

The student will:

LA.5.4.1.1 write narratives that establish a situation and plot with rising action, conflict, and resolution; and

LA.5.4.1.2 write a variety of expressive forms (e.g., fiction, short story, autobiography, science fiction, haiku) that employ figurative language (e.g., simile, metaphor, onomatopoeia, personification, hyperbole), rhythm, dialogue, characterization, plot, and/or appropriate format.

Informative

Standard: The student develops and demonstrates technical writing that provides information related to real-world tasks.

The student will:

LA.5.4.2.1 write in a variety of informational/expository forms (e.g., summaries, procedures, instructions, experiments, rubrics, how-to manuals, assembly instructions);

LA.5.4.2.2 record information (e.g., observations, notes, lists, charts, map labels, legends) related to a topic, including visual aids to organize and record information on charts, data tables, maps and graphs, as appropriate;

LA.5.4.2.3 write informational/expository essays that state a thesis with a narrow focus, contain introductory, body, and concluding paragraphs;

LA.5.4.2.4 write a variety of communications (e.g., friendly letters, thank-you notes, formal letters, messages, invitations) that have a clearly stated purpose and that include the date, proper salutation, body, closing and signature; and

LA.5.4.2.5 write directions to unfamiliar locations using cardinal and ordinal directions, landmarks, and distances, and create an accompanying map.

Persuasive

Standard: The student develops and demonstrates persuasive writing that is used for the purpose of influencing the reader.

The student will write persuasive text (e.g., essay, written communication) that:

LA.5.4.3.1 establish and develop a controlling idea and supporting arguments for the validity of the proposed idea with detailed evidence; and

LA.5.4.3.2 includes persuasive techniques (e.g., word choice, repetition, emotional appeal, hyperbole).

Grade 5: Communication

Penmanship

Standard: The student engages in the writing process and writes to communicate ideas and experiences.

LA.5.5.1.1 The student will demonstrate fluent and legible cursive writing skills.

Listening and Speaking

Standard: The student effectively applies listening and speaking strategies.

The student will:

LA.5.5.2.1 listen and speak to gain and share information for a variety of purposes, including personal interviews, dramatic and poetic recitations, and formal presentations; and

LA.5.5.2.2 make formal oral presentations for a variety of purposes and occasions, demonstrating appropriate language choices, body language, eye contact and the use of gestures, the use of supporting graphics (charts, illustrations, images, props), and available technologies.

Grade 5: Information and Media Literacy

Informational Text

Standard: The student comprehends the wide array of informational text that is part of our day to day experiences.

LA.5.6.1.1 The student will read and interpret informational text and organize the information (e.g., use outlines, timelines, and graphic organizers) from multiple sources for a variety of purposes (e.g., multi-step directions, problem solving, performing a task, supporting opinions, predictions, and conclusions).

Research Process

Standard: The student uses a systematic process for the collection, processing, and presentation of information.

The student will:

LA.5.6.2.1 select a topic for inquiry, formulate a search plan, and apply evaluative criteria (e.g., usefulness, validity, currency, objectivity) to select and use appropriate resources;

LA.5.6.2.2 read and record information systematically, evaluating the validity and reliability of information in text by examining several sources of information;

LA.5.6.2.3 write an informational report that includes a focused topic, appropriate facts, relevant details, a logical sequence, and a concluding statement; and

LA.5.6.2.4 record basic bibliographic data and present quotes using ethical practices (e.g., avoids plagiarism).

Media Literacy

Standard: The student develops and demonstrates an understanding of media literacy as a life skill that is integral to informed decision making.

The student will:

LA.5.6.3.1 examine how ideas are presented in a variety of print and nonprint media and recognize differences between logical reasoning and propaganda; and

LA.5.6.3.2 use a variety of reliable media sources to gather information effectively and to transmit information to specific audiences.

Technology

Standard: The student develops the essential technology skills for using and understanding conventional and current tools, materials and processes.

The student will:

LA.5.6.4.1 select and use appropriate available technologies to enhance communication and achieve a purpose (e.g., video, presentations); and

LA.5.6.4.2 determine and use the appropriate digital tools (e.g., word processing, multimedia authoring, web tools, graphic organizers) for publishing and presenting a topic.